Henry Scott Tuke 1858-1929
Under Canvas

Henry Scott Tuke 1858–1929 Under Canvas

David Wainwright
Catherine Dinn

SAREMA PRESS

Publisher's Note

I was in my teens when I saw my first Tuke painting—*Ruby, Gold, and Malachite* hanging in the Library of the Guildhall in the City of London. In 1985, visiting the Newlyn School Exhibition at the Barbican, I came across the painting again and saw a number of other works by the same artist. I wanted to know more about Henry Scott Tuke but though a biography did exist (written by his sister after his death and published by Martin Secker in 1933) it had long been out of print and there was then nothing more recent. I decided to commission a book that would be both a full length, authoritative biography and an art book that would bring together some of the many Tuke paintings and drawings scattered through public and private collections. This is the book, published on the 60th anniversary of Tuke's death.

The energy, interest and enthusiasm of a great number of people have gone into its publication. I would like to thank most of all the joint authors, David Wainwright and Catherine Dinn. Also Brian Price, an avid collector of photographs, paintings, ephemera and everything pertaining to Tuke's life and work. Over the four years it has taken to put this book together Brian has been an invaluable help and has made the book possible.

I am indebted to Emmanuel Cooper, art critic and author for introducing me to Brian and for his help in the early stages of the project; also to Ian David Baker and to Caroline Fox.

Thanks go to Melissa Denny for the editing, Tim Harvey for the design, my daughters, Sarah and Emma, for the help and support with the research and administrative work involved in a project of this size, and the staff of Gavin Martin Ltd and Sarema Press for their help with production.

I am grateful to Lt-Col Donald Rolph, in his youth one of Tuke's boy models, who shared his memories with me and told wonderful anecdotes. Also to the many owners of Tuke's pictures who allowed our photographers to take over their kitchens, bedrooms and living rooms. In all these cases I can only regret that space considerations did not allow us to use all of the excellent material put at our disposal.

Finally, I would like to express my gratitude to all the museums and galleries that loaned material, but most particularly to Falmouth Art Gallery and to the Tuke Committee of the Royal Cornwall Polytechnic Society, a society with which Tuke himself was actively involved.

If readers know of any other Tuke pictures or photographs, the publishers would be pleased to hear from them in case further material should be published. Some owners who loaned paintings have given us permission to produce postcards of the works. If our readers would be interested in these please contact this company:

Sarema Press (Publishers) Ltd, 15 Beeches Walk, Carshalton, Surrey, SM5 4JS England.

Gordon Rookledge, February 1989

First published in 1989 by Sarema Press (Publishers) Ltd.
Re-printed August 1991

Text © David Wainwright and Catherine Dinn 1989
Photographs and compilation © Sarema Press (Publishers) Ltd., 1989

British Library Cataloguing in Publication Data
Wainwright, David
Henry Scott Tuke: 1858-1929 Under Canvas
1. English paintings, Tuke, Henry Scott. 1858-1929.
Biographies
I Title   II Dinn, Catherine
759.2

ISBN 1 870758 02 1

A Rookledge International Publication

Designed by Tim Harvey
Typeset in Paladium and printed by Mateu Cromo, Spain.

Whilst every effort has been made to secure permission to reproduce photographs, it has in some cases proved impossible. We therefore apologise for any omissions in this respect. When the present whereabouts of significant works are unknown, photographs have sometimes been taken from Tuke's Registers and marked 'present whereabouts unknown' in the caption.

Picture captions: The entry 'R' with a number indicates the appropriate entry in 'The Registers of Henry Scott Tuke' annotated by B. D. Price, Falmouth, Royal Cornwall Polytechnic Society, (2nd Ed.) 1983.

References to the 'Tuke Collection' are to the Tuke Collection of the Royal Cornwall Polytechnic Society (RCPS).

All paintings reproduced, unless otherwise attributed, are by Henry Scott Tuke.

Frontispiece: *Self-portrait*, pastel, 1920 (Royal Institution of Cornwall, Truro, presented by the legatees of Colin Kennedy). Jacket illustrations: (front) detail from *The Run Home* (fig. 69); (back) *Berthe Tresidder* (fig. 50).

Authors' Acknowledgements

The authors wish to thank the Royal Cornwall Polytechnic Society, (owners of the Tuke Collection), the Falmouth Town Council and Art Gallery Committee. They particularly wish to thank Mr Brian D. Price who has with such devotion pursued items concerned with the life and work of H. S. Tuke, and has personally ensured by interviewing over the past 30 years many who were still alive to remember him that such valuable reminiscences have been available to us.

They thank Mrs Ann Willett and Sir Anthony Tuke; Mrs Hilda Trench, Mr John F. Tonkin and Mrs Honor Price; Mr E. G. Dawkins (Town Clerk of Falmouth); Mr Timothy d'Arch Smith; Mr Ronald Smoldon; Mr & Mrs Roger Corfield; Lt-Col Donald Rolph MBE; Mr Arthur Edwards; Mrs Violet Samways; Dr R. Devlin; Dr and Mrs A. J. Dinn; Mr and Mrs A. Shears; Mr Michael Holloway; Mr David Falconer; Mr Peter Rose; Mr Albert Gallichan; Mr Peyton Skipwith (Fine Art Society): Mrs M Blasbery; Mrs F. Cowper-Coles; Miss Bridget Bell; the Librarians of Falmouth Library and the Falmouth School of Art and Design Library, the London Library, and the Norfolk and Norwich Hospital Library; Mrs C. Kelly (Archivist, Royal Geographical Society); Mr Christopher Myers (Secretary, the Arts Club); Mr Michael Richards; Mrs Gwen Mobbs; Mr Richard Tresidder; Mr Neil Miners; Mrs Angela Wright; Mr Alex Hooper; Mr Charles Spicer; Mr and Mrs A. Acton-Page; Mr Julian Hartnoll; Professor John R. Heckenlively; Mr Gerard Irvine; Ms Prudence Cuming; and Mr Andrew Besley; Mr Michael Instone; Mr Jan Channell; Mr S. A. Hosken and the Governors of Falmouth School; Mrs Mary Muirhead; B. D. Jones and B. G. Salisbury; Colmore Galleries and Mrs Susan Exworth

Note on Sources

Certain documents are repeatedly referred to in the Notes, and the following system of abbreviations has been used.

Maria Tuke Sainsbury: *Henry Scott Tuke*, Secker 1933.
This dutiful biography was written by his sister in the years immediately following his death. It makes lavish use of his Diaries, including some that do not seem to have survived, and is therefore a prime source.

REGISTERS Brian D. Price (Editor), 'The Registers of Henry Scott Tuke (1858-1929)', Falmouth: Royal Cornwall Polytechnic Society, 2nd Ed. 1983. Tuke's Registers record his paintings from the time of his first Royal Academy exhibit (1879) to his death. The 'R' numbers have been added by the editor

DIARY 'The Diary of Henry Scott Tuke'
Volume 1, 12 March 1899 to 31 December 1905
Volume 2, 26 November 1923 to 12 July 1925, transcribed by Brian D. Price. Tuke kept diaries throughout his life, but these two volumes appear to be the only ones that have survived.

REMINISCENCES Brian D. Price (Editor), 'Tuke Reminiscences', Falmouth, Royal Cornwall Polytechnic Society, 1983, 68pp. These invaluable interviews were conducted—most in the 1960s—by the editor with twenty-four people who knew the artist or were involved with him.

ARTISTS' LETTERS A collection of letters to and from artists most of whom were contemporary with Tuke, and including some letters to and from the artist. The collection has been assembled and transcribed privately (a copy has been deposited in the National Archive).

Quay scamps, watercolour. 1896 (Tuke Collection, RCPS).

Contents

1. Henry Scott Tuke aged 14. (Private Collection).

Foreword *by Marcia Pointon*

The last decade has seen the serious re-evaluation of Victorian painters whether of the so-called Pre-Raphaelite *avant-garde* or of the mainstream Royal Academy rank and file. We have witnessed a willingness to examine how artworks dismissed as sentimental by our grandparents functioned in the complex and contradictory social structures of the Victorian era. The inclination among some people to embrace Victorian values as well as some, at least, of the features of the Victorian domestic interior may be recognised as a part of this process. But what of the Edwardians? Admittedly, galleries are gradually recovering the paintings of this era from their storage areas and presenting once again for public view the bequests of a generation that we might be forgiven for thinking— based on this evidence—spent its time boating, playing cricket and croquet and picnicking. Even the term 'Edwardian' still evokes for most of us a one-sided fading world of gossip and garden parties, of family fortunes fractured on the Somme.

Clausen, Lavery, Gwen John, and her brother Augustus John, have all attracted attention in recent years. The commissioned war artists and those declared modern by Roger Fry and Clive Bell have never dropped from sight. But Henry Scott Tuke—like Georgian poetry, monocles and parasols—seemed perhaps too securely lodged in the forgettable compartment of Edwardianism to merit serious attention outside, at least, of his home of Falmouth. It is here where many of his best-known and loved paintings were executed that the major collection of his work as well as manuscript material charting his professional life has been kept. The fact that he recommended his heirs to hold on to the paintings he bequeathed them signals less his self-esteem than his business sense and his awareness that his paintings seemed old-fashioned by the time of his death in 1929.

We think of Tuke as the painter of bathing boys, which, indeed, he was. Yet his repertoire— as this biography demonstrates—is a great deal wider than this reputation would imply. A close look at, say, *All Hands to the Pumps!* (now in the National Maritime Museum) rapidly dispels any lingering disposition to regard Tuke as exclusively devoted to the *plein-air* male adolescent nude. This is a work of bold composition, a view of labour, vigorously painted as a drama of daily life, albeit marine daily life. Looking at such large scale work with its free but confident handling of paint and its restrained palette it is easy now to understand the reputation commanded by Tuke in his maturity both in Britain and across the channel in France.

Yet what of the paintings of boys bathing that Henry Scott Tuke continued to produce whether in Falmouth, Jamaica or Italy until the end of his life? Our own age has recently shown renewed concern with the Great War, its histories, literature and mythologies, and with the class specific lifestyles and sexual orientation of those who were young men and women in the years leading up to 1914. The 'new chivalry' of Tuke's friend Kains Jackson with its 'exultation of the youthful masculine ideal' needs to be seen alongside the patriotism of Rupert Brooke. And that patriotism with its cult of masculine beauty should not be dissociated from a cultural milieu in which Tuke posed his boy models (his 'quay scamps') on the Cornish beaches, careful to protect them from the over-enthusiastic admiration of some of his house guests as well as from the sun which threatened to spoil the flesh-tones he strove to represent on canvas. Such paintings— like the sensual imagery of Caravaggio or the passionate letters of Vita Sackville-West—need no apology. They are not only evidence of Tuke's particular penchant and of his ability to translate a pre-occupation into vivid pictorial form, they are part of a continuing material culture that lends public form to the private and often proscribed search for perfection.

It is, therefore, opportune that this full-length and thoroughly documented biography should be published now. Titles like *Lovers of the Sun* and *Morning Splendour* should not deter the historian or the serious viewer. Tuke's work is symptomatic of a significant episode of late nineteenth- and early twentieth-century history. His painting draws on the continental experience learned from Alphonse Legros and Bastien-Lepage. Part of an extended network of friends which included Lord Ronald Gower and John Addington Symonds, Tuke was connected with the foundation of the New English Art Club and the formation of the Newlyn School. Moreover, the very conservatism of his style and the insistent reiteration of his paintings' envisioned world of sun and sea are meaningful reminders of the power that the idyll of unchanging youthful health and strength possessed over a class, a generation and perhaps a nation.

2.   Tuke painting *The Embarcation* on the beach at Swanpool, *c.*1912. The colour photograph was taken by George Beldam (Private Collection).

CHAPTER ONE
The Bathing Place

When Harry Tuke was twelve years old and living at Falmouth he and his brother Willie, two years his senior, were taught to swim by a young Cambridge don[1] who was in the town to lecture at their father's invitation. Their bathing place was Sunny Cove, a cleft in the rocks at Pennance, the stretch of coast enclosing the south-western end of Falmouth Bay. It was approachable then, as now, only by boat or by a perilous path winding down the rocks and covered with tangled undergrowth. Sunny Cove appealed to the boys of Falmouth because they could strip off and bathe un-trammelled in the clear blue-green sea, then lie on the beach and watch the great sailing-ships as they cut through the sea, heading round Pendennis Point towards Falmouth Harbour, or furled their sails and dropped anchor in the Bay as they waited to dock and discharge their cargoes.

That sight of the sea, the sun, the sand and relaxed young men in such a naturally beautiful setting, with, in the middle distance, the great ships of the last triumphant days of sail, etched itself unforgettably on young Harry Tuke's memory. He was to return to Falmouth and paint those scenes again and again. Although he made a parallel and distinguished reputation as a portraitist, he would have been the first to recog-

nise that 'a typical Tuke' meant Sunny Cove, and the beaches to either side of it: Newporth to the south, and the strip of sand below the cliff-top cottage that was to become known in Falmouth as 'Tuke's Beach'.

Henry Scott Tuke was born in York on 12 June 1858, the younger son of Dr Daniel Hack Tuke, consultant to the Friends' Retreat. Dr Tuke was a leader of the Quaker community to which his family had belonged for at least four generations. His great-grandfather, William Tuke (1732-1822), had founded the Friends' Retreat, far ahead of its time in its sensitive and intelligent treatment of the mentally ill. Daniel Hack Tuke had married Esther Maria Stickney of Holderness, Lincolnshire; her mother had come from another York Quaker family, the Mennells. Daniel Tuke had willingly taken up the family tradition of caring for psychiatric patients, and was earning a national reputation for his published studies of insanity. It seemed that the family would remain in York, and two sons were born there: William Samuel Tuke in 1856, and Henry Scott Tuke two years later (his middle name was the maiden name of his paternal great-grandmother). Then in 1859 Dr Tuke began to betray symptoms of incipient tuberculosis. He was obliged to give up his prac-

3. Irwin Sharp's Friends' Boarding School at Weston-super-Mare, c 1872. Tuke is seated third from the right. (Private Collection).

tice and move his young family south to a milder climate.

They travelled first to Clevedon, in Somerset; then in 1860 they moved to Falmouth. It was a place with a number of Quaker families, notably the Fox family who became close friends—Robert Were Fox at Penjerrick, and Alfred Lloyd Fox at Penmere. In this congenial haven a daughter, named Maria, was born to the Tukes in 1861.

Harry Tuke's boyhood in Falmouth seems to have been unclouded. The children were taught by governesses, then the boys went to a tutor, and finally they were sent to the Friends' School at Weston-super-Mare. School does not seem to have made a great impact upon Harry (although Arthur Tanner, who also became an artist, remained a friend from this time). It is apparent that a much greater influence was his home, from which he derived his love of books and of classical music. His sister Maria describes those years:

We profited much by the culture of our parents, both of whom were widely read and keenly interested in literature, history, politics—everything. They were strongly religious but without narrowness, very clear in their canons of right and wrong, but full of understanding and sympathy for young people who suffered from a narrow upbringing . . . Both loved poetry, and Mrs Tuke was always easily moved by romance, old ballads, and singing. She read aloud to us by the hour, while we did wool-work or knitting or drawing. She was of an equable temperament with a keen sense of humour, shrewd and sometimes caustic. They both had a gift for making friends readily. Dr Tuke was a strong Liberal and the boys became ardent partisans for the same cause . . . Harry always remained a Liberal, having the greatest admiration for Gladstone, and later for Asquith.

The life in Falmouth was a very healthy and happy one, with many occupations besides lessons: stamp-collecting (a long-continued hobby), butterfly-chasing, drawing and painting, chess, long walks, bathing, and visiting at Quaker and other houses . . . They would give us what Harry called 'Quaker soup', a wonderful white decoction, based on chicken and cream and almonds . . .[2]

Croquet was a great game then, played in the old style, and Harry was one of the people who could play without losing his temper. There was also what was called 'going on the water', but as that was the last thing either parent wished to do, we had little of it, beyond an annual picnic to Trefusis.[3]

During those Falmouth years Dr Tuke regained his strength, continued his studies and writings on mental health, and became actively involved with the Working Men's Club, the Friends' Adult School and the Public Library. Meanwhile Harry drew and drew.

[His] letters were always full of little drawings, as when there was an epidemic of smallpox in the town he drew a girl he had seen fully out in the spots. In others there was a militia-man in his tent, a cuckoo cuckooing, and 'l'Empereur', when Napoleon III came as an exile to Chislehurst . . . Ships . . . always fascinated him. In those days the bay and the harbour were always peopled with sailing ships and clumsy-looking steamers with paddles. He must have seen the tea-clippers passing on the horizon— probably the Cutty Sark in all her glory—and some that came in for repairs, as I think the Sir Lancelot did in 1866. The Great Eastern went by on one occasion, and there is a drawing of nine men-of-war all at once . . . The ships coming in and out, the sun rising across the bay, and every change of weather and season along that rocky coast were more to him than all the interests and pleasures of town.[4]

In the summer of 1874 Willie Tuke was eighteen. He had decided, to his father's satisfaction, to become a doctor and had been accepted as a medical student at University College, London. Because of this, Dr Tuke felt that the family must leave Falmouth and establish themselves in London. It may also be that, with the improvement in his own health, he thought this a good opportunity to move closer to the mainstream of his own profession.

The family took rooms first in Fitzroy Square, and then—partly to provide room for Harry, who left school in December—at 5 Charlotte Street, Bedford Square (the house was subsequently renumbered 30 Bloomsbury Street). There was then the problem of what to do about Harry, now sixteen years old. There was family discussion and the older relations considered that he would be wise to take the place offered to him in his uncle's bank at Hitchin. He was not entirely against that proposal, but on balance decided that he wished to go to art school. To some of the older Quaker relatives this smacked of frivolousness. It was distressing to Dr Tuke, who wrote to Dr Blanche, father of Jacques-Emile, the painter, in France lamenting that their sons should both adopt such unprofessional pursuits.[5] A year or two later, when he had achieved a showing in the

Royal Academy, an old West Country Quaker lady pointedly asked him: 'Does *thy* father quite concur in *thy* profession?'

However, Dr and Mrs Tuke were very supportive and in January 1875 Henry Scott Tuke entered the Slade School. His school friends Arthur Tanner and Cecil Wedmore were in London studying for business, but Henry Tuke was never slow to make friends and he was soon a popular figure with his fellow-students at the Slade, whose Professor at that time was F. J. Poynter (afterwards Sir Edward Poynter, Director of the National Gallery and President of the Royal Academy). Among Tuke's particular friends were Joseph Benwell Clark, William Strang, and George Jacomb-Hood. But the catalyst figure of that generation seems to have been Thomas Cooper Gotch.

4. Dr Daniel Hack Tuke (left) with his sons, Henry Scott Tuke and William Samuel Tuke, Torquay, 1879. (Private Collection).

The friendship between Tuke and Gotch may have been strengthened by the number of things they had in common. Although Gotch was older than the general run of students—he was twenty-four at this time—like Tuke he came from a nonconformist family with links with banking. He therefore shared with Tuke an appreciation of non-conformity, and a broad cultural background. After a few years working in his father's boot and shoe business he had left it, at twenty-two, to study at Heatherly's art studio, transferring to the Slade just as Tuke joined.[6] At Heatherly's he had been a friend of Charles Gogin and Samuel Butler, the author of *Erewhon*.

Gotch was one of the friends with whom Henry Tuke would go for long walks in the country. But in Tuke's first years at the Slade, where he was an assiduous student, most of his spare time was spent with his family. On Sundays he would walk with his parents, brother and sister to the Quaker meeting in Westminster. In the afternoon he and his sister Maria would go to Westminster Abbey or St Paul's to listen to the music; and on Sunday evenings Dr Tuke would take his family to hear some leading non-conformist preacher. Henry Tuke would visit the British Museum and the National Gallery, or go to hear Gladstone speaking in the House of Commons. Very fond of music, he would take his mother to ballad concerts. The holidays were usually spent with Tuke relations, in Hull (where he played cricket and croquet), York, Southport, Hitchin, Exeter (the Mennells) or Torquay. There were also occasional summer visits to Falmouth. Christmas was spent at Saffron Walden, either with the Gibsons (Mrs George Gibson was a Tuke aunt) or in the homes of William or James Tuke.[7]

In the summer of 1877 the new Slade Professor, Alphonse Legros (a Frenchman, who had come to London as a refugee from the Paris Commune), awarded Henry Tuke the Slade scholarship, which gave him £50 a year for three years. That summer he went abroad for the first time, with a schoolfriend, A. H. Wallis, visiting Belgium, the field of the Battle of Waterloo, and then Paris. A year later he went on a walking tour in Normandy with another schoolfriend, Arthur Tanner, and then took his mother to Paris to see the Exhibition, where 'he was much struck with the French manner of painting'.[8]

He was still searching for an artistic ideal; in the previous summer, he had particularly admired Burne-Jones and Whistler in the first exhibition at the Grosvenor Gallery. It was at this time that he took a share of H. M. Paget's studio, together with Tom Gotch and Benwell Clark. In February 1879, with his fellow student Harold Rathbone (a

relative of Paget) he visited the studio of Burne-Jones, noting that 'truly he is the most marvellous of all modern painters'.[9]

His first public success came in the Royal Academy Summer Exhibition of 1879, when shortly before his twenty-first birthday he heard that a painting and an etching had been accepted. The painting was an imitation 'Old Master', entitled *The Good Samaritan* and in later years he was much ashamed of it. His mother, naturally, was immensely proud of it and hung it where she could always see it. Harry was more satisfied with his small etching, of William Strang, which he called *The Highland Boy*.

That summer the Tuke family were lent the house of an uncle at Torquay. After travelling down from London with them, Harry went on to Falmouth in company with Tom Gotch, to sketch, fish and bathe. Having passed twenty-one, it looks as though Harry was trying his wings and beginning to fly the family nest. A letter to his father at this time implies that he was rejecting paternal advice on some matter;[10] but there is no indication of the precise nature of the difference between them. Writing to Tom Gotch that summer, Jane Ross (one of their fellow-students), remarks that another friend, Carrie Yates, 'is at

Newlyn, near Penzance. I can't remember much about the relative positions of Penzance and Falmouth'.[11] Within a few years the art world was to learn.

In the autumn, Willie, who had turned republican and revolutionary (to his father's undisguised irritation) had founded, with his friend Victor Horsley, a club (sometimes known as the 'Pioneers'), where 'scientists' and medical students, friends of Willie such as Harrington Sainsbury, would meet with art students — Tuke, Gotch and their friends — for 'Free Discussion and Social Intercourse'. There were to be some twenty members, and they would hold to the determination 'not to contradict or confute, nor to believe and take for granted, nor to find talk and discourse, but to weigh and consider'.[12] Though the club met on a number of occasions (and on one occasion listened to a paper from the ubiquitous Tom Gotch on 'Life, an Art'), its principles frightened off some of the more refined young ladies, who were apprehensive that discussion about 'free love', a powerful topic among social radicals of the period, might become too dangerous. The future of the club was also imperilled when, that autumn, its founder Willie Tuke, having passed his medical examinations

5. Portrait of Edith and Gertrude Santley with Carrie Yates, oil, 1880. R3. (York City Art Gallery). Exhibited at the Royal Academy in 1880 but dated 1884.

with distinction, was tragically found to be suffering from the same tubercular condition as his father, and was obliged to take a job as a medical attendant to a rich young man wintering in the drier climate of Egypt.

Two female members of the club, and fellow-students with Harry at the Slade, were Gertrude and Edith Santley. They were the daughters of Charles Santley (later Sir Charles), the leading baritone in oratorio and opera in London—and also an enthusiastic artist. From autumn 1879 he joined his daughters at the Slade but proved an unpromising student. An early experience for him there was to be required to study Harry Tuke's portrait of his brother Willie, which was highly praised by Professor Legros. It was no penance, for the whole Santley family had taken to Harry: 'I do love that boy', said the father.[13] He carried his affection to the length of giving Harry and Tom Gotch singing lessons, free, in Paget's studio. His house in Upper Hamilton Terrace, St John's Wood, became a second London home to Tuke.

After Christmas 1879 Harry abandoned his family at Saffron Walden and went skating at the Welsh Harp, Hendon, with the Santley girls and their friend Carrie Yates. Evidently there was some ulterior motive behind this, for he wrote to Tom Gotch:

6. Portrait of Maria Tuke, oil on panel, 1881. (Private Collection).

> I received only one Xmas card, but ah! who was that one from, do you think. I daresay you can guess; it hoped that 'joy and fair content might crown me through the year', which part she has underlined. I am painting her a New Year's one of some demi-classical people skating, and Cupid coming up behind, rather Gotchine in subject, and a small sequel to it, where they have all fallen into the water, which (with your permission) I may send to Bosy [Gertrude]. Of course it has no reference to anything that might take place at Hendon.[14]

It can be deduced from this that Harry was proposing at least a flirtation with Edith Santley, while Tom Gotch was making up to her sister, Gertrude. This is confirmed by a letter from Benwell Clark to Gotch following an end-of-year skating party at Hendon in which he hopes that the letter will find Gotch 'struggling with, and overcoming Cupid'.[15]

Whatever the intention, nothing positive transpired. Perhaps Edith Santley was one of the girls of whom Harry said to his sister Maria, 'That is the only girl I could have married'—a phrase she says (with an affectionate sister's amusement) he used to her 'three or four times'.[16] Perhaps he sublimated his affections, as so often, in work. For that spring, as a gift from Mrs Santley to her husband, he painted a portrait of the Santley girls and Carrie Yates. Edith stands apart from the other two girls, holding a musical score, her lips slightly parted in song. It is a dramatic effect, and has a vitality derived from a deep feeling for the sitters. It was hung in the Royal Academy in 1880, and it is said that Leighton went up to it at the hanging committee and asked: 'Can it be an old master?' It could not, he said, be by a young man.

Samuel Butler, radical, free-thinker, was called by his young girl fellow-students at Heatherly's 'the incarnate bachelor'.[17] He was then forty-five, living in Clifford's Inn, where he was frequently in the company of his younger friend, Henry Festing Jones. He knew some of the Slade students through his friendship with Charles Gogin and Tom Gotch, the latter being something of a favourite with Butler. Evidently he heard about Tuke from Festing Jones, who had been introduced to him by Gotch and found him 'delightful'.[18] A meeting was arranged at Clifford's Inn, at which Butler discovered that Tuke shared his devotion to the music of Handel. In February 1880 Butler was once again trying to persuade Gotch to bring Tuke to see him, if necessary with Benwell Clark: 'I like Clark too but not half as much as I like you and Tuke'.[19]

During this spring, the success of the Santley picture drew Harry Tuke still closer to the family. Generously, Charles Santley invited him to go with them on their summer holiday in Italy. He accepted. Before he set off, he seems (naively) to have confided to Samuel Butler his affection for Edith Santley. 'The incarnate bachelor' was horror struck. Butler's friends could have told Tuke that when his friends married, he generally dropped them (one rare exception was Charles Gogin). In the chronology of his life, he writes at one point that 'About this time McCullock got married and began so far as I am concerned to cease to exist'.[20]

Butler was also travelling in Italy that summer, and in July and August wrote letters to Tuke begging him not to get engaged, or if he had done so, to break off the engagement. Gotch may have told Butler that he was considering proposing to Tuke's sister, Maria, for he was now thrust beyond the pale:

Don't bring Gotch to see me any more. If you want to see me on your return either come alone, or with Jones or with Paget, but I am tired of Gotch and don't want him any more.[21]

Tuke's art was to bring him into contact with numbers of emotional bachelors: he was early exposed to the experience. But with Harry's customary good-humour the crisis seems to have been overcome; not least, no doubt, because Harry had not proceeded with any engagement, and probably never proposed, for he continued from time to time to visit Clifford's Inn for Handel and conversation with Butler and Festing Jones.

On his return from Italy, after two calls on members of the family, Tuke went down to Falmouth. The ostensible reason was to move some of the family's stored possessions from a damp stable-loft to a dry ship's-biscuit store owned by the Downing family, who had become his good friends. He returned in October to finish a portrait commission before setting off to spend the winter in Florence—another new experience.

In the autumn of 1880 Maria, now nineteen, again asked to join her brother at the Slade school as an art student. Her parents would not allow it, however; their daughter must be protected from the wild life. Harry argued her case but could not move his parents. Tom Gotch was drawn in, and wrote a letter to Mrs Tuke that was evidently regarded as impertinent by the older generation. Willie was obliged to tell Gotch not to visit them in Ambleside because of the 'feeling roused against you in the authorities of this household'.[22] Maria took the matter more calmly, writing to Jessie Gotch:

Harry amused me, he said he lookt (*sic*) forward to when we are all about 40, to having a good time, and being quite independent; I thought it would be rather hard to wait till then before one had one's fun, but it will be all the more festive when it does come.[23]

Harry planned to spend the winter studying in Italy, only delaying his departure in order to fulfil a commission to paint a posthumous portrait of John Ford, the former Headmaster of the Friends' School at York.

That completed, he set off across a snow-clad Europe, breaking his journey for a few days in Paris to meet his friends from the Slade now ensconced in the studios of the fashionable teachers, Laurens and Julien. Then he travelled on to Florence, where he took rooms in a modest *pensione* overlooking the Ponte Vecchio, and obtained a pass authorising him to copy old masters in the major galleries. Always willing to listen to advice, he was guided by a Florentine teacher, Acquarolli — 'one of the many who know how Titian painted, and he says everything was modelled in green first: "*tutto verde, tutto verde, tutto verde*"[24]. Harry tried it in a self-portrait, and then attempted a copy of Titian's *Flora* on this principle, reporting in a letter to Gotch: 'it looks ghastly at present and is the horror of all the visitors'.[25]

He was also busy on a picture for submission to the Royal Academy in the following spring. There was little enough time, not least because he had also obtained permission to join the life class in the Florentine Academy. He was also making friends and acquaintances through the introductions provided by his friends in London. He took up what was to prove the most important on 30 November, when on the recommendation of his Slade friend H. M. Paget (a member of the British family prominent in the Florentine artistic community) he visited Arthur Lemon and his wife.

Arthur Lemon was eight years older than Harry Tuke. He was a 'man's man', and a powerful advocate of *plein air* painting. Born in the Isle of Man, he had grown up with relatives in Rome. When it seemed likely that he would be drawn into soldiering with Garibaldi, he took ship for America and spent eight years as a cowboy and cattle-herder, before returning to Italy and painting.[26] He and Harry took to each other at once. Harry wrote to Carrie Yates of his friends in Florence:

Mr Lemon, Paget's friend, I must certainly put first: I hope I have not squeezed him too hard, but he is a perfect reservoir of juice, in the shape of always having some plan to assist one when in difficulties.[27]

One of Lemon's plans was to direct Harry towards a much cheaper lodging, brick-floored and unheated, but he also hired a heated studio. There he worked on his Royal Academy picture. At first it was going to be a big street scene based on an old orange-man with a blue cloak; but then at Lemon's suggestion he embarked on something smaller, a *bronzista* shop, 'merely a scene in the mercato, a group before a brass lamp and pot shop, but it is in its subtle combinations that its interest, if successful, will lie. The figures are life size, half-length'.[28]

Considering that time was short and he was still unsettled in his surroundings this was an over-ambitious plan, and his changing views under Lemon's influence did not make for self-confidence. He was very well aware of this, writing to his sister Maria:

I painted the brass pots and lamps so much better than all the rest that the heads had to be done nearly all over again. They are much better now but only after a desperate struggle. I am going in heavily for naturalism now, this picture will never be very good as it will bear evident marks of the failure of the old style, and an insufficient experience of the new, but now I am beginning to have a new faith I shall not mind so much. It is a very odd thing that I have been much more influenced since I came here by Mr Lemon than by the old masters. He is a first-rater. I hope you will see him some day. He can tell you almost to a T what is wrong with a picture, so I get him to come round pretty often.[29]

Always professional, Harry continued working at the picture, but was increasingly drawn to the visual delights of Italy. He wrote to Gotch:

I feel in a considerable state of excitement about painting just at present . . . You must come here before long; it is the land of inspiration . . . The gradation of the sky is something astonishing, this evening almost the whole strength of the palette. The most beautiful effect is about half an hour after sunset, when the sky opposite the sun becomes a mysterious grey blue, quite unlike anything I ever saw in England . . . My picture which I had almost thought of giving up in the early part of the week, has had quite a revival in consequence of my painting some potty things on

the plan; the shiny metal gives great value to the flesh. I am with you that things ought to be painted as much as possible from the object.[30]

But painting pots and pans, however technically challenging, was not satisfying enough, and he added: 'I feel I must have another long spell at the nude before long, in some place where I shall not be disturbed and where models are cheap'.[31]

The picture was finished. It was crated and dispatched to London in mid March. A few weeks later commiserations were arriving, for Tuke's *Bronzista Shop* had been rejected by the Academy. Perhaps he was not unduly surprised, though disappointed. At least he was in good company, for Gotch and Benwell Clark were also rejected, as was Arthur Lemon. It was a sweet and sour summer for Tom Gotch. Earlier in the year he had written to Dr Hack Tuke asking permission to propose to Maria. Given permission, he had proposed and been accepted. He then had second thoughts, and in May he wrote to Dr Tuke asking to withdraw. Dr Tuke accepted his withdrawal, asking only that he send a letter to Maria by the hands of Willie, so that Maria would not have to read it at a family breakfast table.[32] All this was done with civility. Maria did not show her grief. Years later she told her granddaughter that she had truly loved Tom Gotch, and that his departure had been one of the two profound sorrows of her life.[33] The reason for Gotch's withdrawal became apparent when in June he became engaged to his fellow-student in Paris, Carrie Yates. They visited his parents in Kettering, and then went down to Newlyn where they married on 31 August.[34]

At the beginning of June, Harry Tuke and Arthur Lemon went to the coast, the 'blue and festive Mediterranean'[35] as Harry described it. In the village of Pietra Santa, near Forte dei Marmi between Leghorn and Spezia, lived Charles Heath Wilson, one of the great figures in Florentine art circles. Then in his early seventies, he had lived in Italy for twelve years, mainly painting water-colours, after a distinguished career first as a teacher of ornament and design in Edinburgh, then as director of the Art Schools at Somerset House in London, and finally as head of the Glasgow School of Design. His biography of Michelangelo had been published two years earlier, in 1879. He was also advisor to the American artist John Singer Sargent and his family.[36] For Harry Tuke he was, like Lemon, 'a most congenial companion'. Tuke wrote to Gotch:

This place . . . is one of the principal places for shipping the marble from the quarries in the

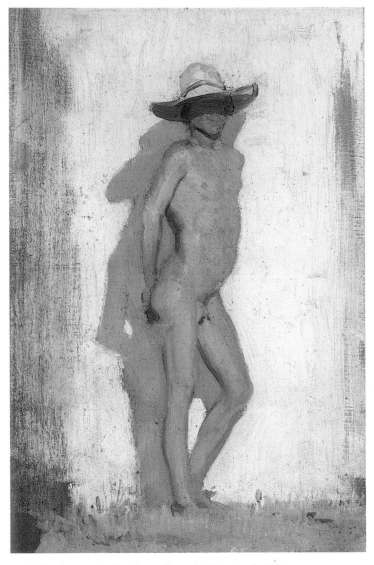

7.   *Italian boy on the beach near Forte dei Marmi*, oil, 1881.
(Collection Michael Holloway and David Falconer).

8.   Arthur Lemon: *Italian boy on the beach near Forte dei Marmi,* oil, 1881.
(Collection Michael Holloway and David Falconer).

mountains behind us, per consequence there are splendid things to be seen in the way of white bullocks pulling heavy loads, and men lading ships. We are going to paint nude boys on the shore in a few days. We began yesterday in a small way by sketching one in the sea, but the approach of females put a stop to further operations. Both these men are great tonists so I hope to learn lots.[37]

His four weeks on the coast were blissful. He had discovered the way of life that suited him. In the sea, the sun and the sand, providing a setting for paintings done from life, and in the open air, he discovered the mix of elements that was to provide him with fruitful success. His sister Maria recognised this from his letters; as she wrote when she came to describe it all later:

He was perfectly happy, and felt that at last he had found what he really wanted to do . . . He loved the outdoor life, with its combination of painting, bathing, boating and congenial companionship, and the people of the place charmed him, as he evidently charmed them. Some of the boys wrote to him afterwards, addressing him as 'Stimatissimo Signor Enrico,' and he composed Italian letters to them— Aristide, Oreste, Egidio, Lorenzo, Canfino— all their names fascinated him, and they escorted him as far as they could, when on July 11 he most regretfully tore himself away. Heath Wilson wrote in December 1881: 'I got your letter at the old place, Forte dei Marmi, and very pleased all the people were to hear news of Signor Tuke. You can have no idea of how your memory is loved and reverenced by old and young there.'[38]

From the time of his first Royal Academy success in 1879 Tuke kept a Register in which he recorded where and when his pictures were painted, to whom they were sold and at what price, where they went to, and (when the information came to his notice) when, where and at what price they were re-sold. It is a meticulous catalogue, but not exhaustive since he did not include his many sketches or experimental works. His record of this Italian visit does not, for instance, list the *Bronzista Shop*, nor does it list the beach pictures, though he certainly brought some back. He lists two Florentine townscapes, one of the Ponte Vecchio (which he gave to his mother) and one of the market, which was sold for £10 less 10 percent. He brought back one copy, of Titian's *Holy Family with St Anthony* in the Uffizi Gallery. Charles Santley paid him £50 for it, and gave it to the St Joseph's Retreat in Highgate.[39]

1 Maria Tuke Sainsbury: *Henry Scott Tuke*, Secker 1933, p.21. He was Frederic W. H. Myers (1843-1901), then a lecturer in classics at Trinity College, Cambridge; subsequently an Inspector of Schools, and founder of the Society for Psychical Research

2 'Quaker soup' is clearly a survival of the 18th century 'white soup' beloved of Jane Austen, though with chicken substituted for gammon. See Jane Grigson: 'Food with the Famous', Penguin 1979, pp.66-70

3 Maria Tuke Sainsbury, pp.18-20

4 Maria Tuke Sainsbury, pp.21-22

5 Conversation (DW) with Mrs Ann Willett, 17 June 1987

6 C. Fox and F. Greenacre: *Painting in Newlyn*, Barbican Art Gallery 1985, p.75

7 Maria Tuke Sainsbury, pp.24-27

8 Maria Tuke Sainsbury, pp.28-30

9 Maria Tuke Sainsbury, p.32

10 Maria Tuke Sainsbury, p.34

11 Artists' Letters: Jane Ross to T. C. Gotch, 23 Aug 1879, No.48

12 Artists' Letters: Gertrude Sainsbury to T. C. Gotch, 2 Feb 1881, No.122

13 Maria Tuke Sainsbury, p.44

14 Artists' Letters: Henry Scott Tuke to T. C. Gotch, 28 Dec 1879, No.77

15 Artists' Letters: J. Benwell Clark to T. C. Gotch, 30 Dec 1879, No.79

16 Maria Tuke Sainsbury, p.43

17 H. Festing Jones: *Samuel Butler, a Memoir*

18 Artists' Letters: Samuel Butler to T. C. Gotch, n.d., No.81

19 Artists' Letters: Samuel Butler to T. C. Gotch, 29 Feb 1880, No.84

20 Philip Henderson: *Samuel Butler*, Cohen & West 1953, p.94

21 Maria Tuke Sainsbury, p.42

22 Artists' Letters: W. S. Tuke to T. C. Gotch, 1 Sept 1880, No.108

23 Artists' Letters: Maria Tuke Sainsbury to J. Gotch, 8 Oct 1880, No.110

24 Artists' Letters: Henry Scott Tuke to T. C. Gotch, 22 Dec 1880, No.117

25 *ibid*

26 Stanley Olson: *John Singer Sargent*, Macmillan 1986, p.30

27 Artists' Letters: Henry Scott Tuke to C. B. Yates, 16 Jan 1881, No.120

28 *ibid*

29 Maria Tuke Sainsbury, p.48

30 Artists' Letters: Henry Scott Tuke to T. C. Gotch, 11 Feb 1881, No.127

31 *ibid*

32 Artists' Letters: Daniel H. Tuke to T. C. Gotch, 19 May 1881, No.139

33 Conversation (DW) with Mrs Ann Willett, 17 June 1987

34 C. Fox and F. Greenacre: *Painting in Newlyn*, Barbican Art Gallery 1985, p.76

35 Artists' Letters: Henry Scott Tuke to T. C. Gotch, 6 June 1881, No.141

36 Stanley Olson, *John Singer Sargent*, op.cit.

37 Artists' Letters: Henry Scott Tuke to T. C. Gotch, 6 June 1881, No.141

38 Maria Tuke Sainsbury, p.52

39 Henry Scott Tuke Registers (R8). It is still there

9.   Portrait of Arthur Lemon, oil, *c.*1881. (Collection Michael Holloway and David Falconer).

10.   Chevallier Tayler and Tuke, Newlyn, *c.*1883. (Private Collection).

CHAPTER TWO
Paris and Newlyn

A period of study in Paris was a logical progression after the Slade. Indeed, several of Tuke's fellow-students had already gone there, Tom Gotch and Carrie Yates among them. Tuke wrote to Gotch from Florence in March 1881 saying that he would probably spend the next winter in Paris and asking: 'What is your more matured opinion of Laurens' atelier as a place to work in? Is it adapted to four or five months' steady practice? I saw a large picture of Laurens' here today, the death of some military swell, with much chef in it'.[1] (The word *chef*, a favourite with Tuke at this time, is used to mean 'good' or 'desirable'). Gotch replied a few weeks later:

> I wouldn't change myself, tho' the work is not very good. I like Laurens; he is very original in composition and interests himself in it. The noise, the heat, the smoke, and the students generally, depress me beyond measure, and I am played out pretty soon every day; but one learns.[2]

Jean Paul Laurens was a leading teacher in Paris at that time, and places in his studio were much sought after. He was a painter of large formal pictures in the tragic manner, a French tradition dating back to David. But Laurens was acknowledged to be a proficient painter, and a good teacher. Gotch arranged for Tuke to be given an introduction through a member of the studio, Emile Tremblay. In October 1881 Tuke presented himself at Laurens' *atelier* and was accepted.

For the first few weeks his friends in England complained that he was concentrating so single-mindedly on his work that they heard nothing of him. Then, gradually, he began to pick up the threads of a social life. This was not difficult, since his fellow-student George Jacomb-Hood took a room next to his on the top floor of a little hotel (the Hotel Odessa) in Montparnasse, overlooking the railway station square, and 'noisy with the clatter of omnibuses and the neighing of their grey Percheron horses'.[3] The two of them used to join William Strang and Joe Benwell Clark for a meat tea at Gatti's and then spend an evening in a theatre gallery. Other former Slade students in Paris were Alexander Chevallier Tayler, Fred Millard, Oswald von Glehn and the Scot James Paterson (all at the Laurens studio). Tuke was necessarily careful with money at this period, and he and Jacomb-Hood discovered a cabmen's bar under Montparnasse station where they could eat cheaply and well.[4]

Tuke's doctor father had provided him with several introductions to the leading French specialists in mental illness, among whom his published work had a high reputation. As hungry students are glad to do in such circumstances, Harry took up the introductions and fortunately found himself launched on a series of pleasant new friendships. One doctor, Foville, held a dinner for him, at which he met another, Dr Bouchereau. The latter asked him home a few days later: 'He lives with his aged mother and homely sister, so we had a very comfortable easy time, and the best meal I have had for long, more substantial than the dinner, which was all courses of little snips, mere tinkering'.[5] On these occasions he was eager to practise his French, which he began to speak well. Jacomb-Hood recalled that Tuke would retire to his little room before such a visit, and could be heard 'with his usual thoroughness spending an hour or so before going, reading aloud to himself some French author, to get his tongue accustomed to the accent'.[6]

He was also introduced, probably by Gotch, to a young American artist building a considerable reputation as a portraitist, particularly among his expatriate fellow-countrymen and women who, ten years after the horrors of the Commune when Paris was closed to visitors and tourists, were now flocking to the capital of culture. Sociable and gregarious, only two years older than Tuke but widely travelled in Europe, John Singer Sargent soon became a good friend. It was said of him that somehow he was never in a hurry to get to his studio, and always had time for visitors. On his first encounter Tuke was shown 'lots of fine sketches', and met the subject of Sargent's current portrait, the statesman Clemenceau. Evidently taken with the young Englishman, Sargent invited him to lunch the next day, then to a concert at the Berlioz Festival. Tuke was a little overawed:

> I think I shall gather a good deal from Sargent, he is much the most talented of all my acquaintances. His sketches in Italy and Spain are something to marvel at, colour, tone and drawing all united. I think I shall like him, but at first I felt he was too polished and suave to become very intimate with, he made me feel I did not know what to do with my hands. He is not quite 26 and is up to his ears in portraits.[7]

Tuke spent Christmas Day rambling through the woods near Versailles with John Julius Huybers, an Australian fellow-student with Laurens. Early in the New Year, 1882, he paid another studio visit, to Bastien-Lepage, where he 'saw many things of surpassing beauty'.[8] This provided a great contrast to the Laurens studio, for Jules Bastien-Lepage was bracketed with Manet and Millet as a leader of the movement to take art out of the studio and the academies, and liberate it in the open air. As Stanhope Forbes described the movement:

> Most of us young students were turning our backs on the great cities, forsaking the studios with their unvarying north light, to set up our easels in country districts, where we could pose our models and attack our work in sunshine or in shadow, under the open sky.[9]

Another strong influence on Tuke at this time was the American Alexander Harrison, who with his brother, Birge, was a leader of the expatriate artists' colonies at Grez-sur-Loing, south-east of Paris, and at Pont Aven and Concarneau in Brittany. These groups greatly admired the *plein air* painting of Bastien-Lepage; but it was Harrison who broke new ground by persuading small boys and then girl models to pose nude for him out-of-doors. Harrison's preference was for settings of natural beauty — the beach (as in *The Wave*) or the orchard (*In Arcadia*), both painted in 1884-5; and he tended to be ironic about his fellow-artists who chose to paint the social realism of the fishing port: it was Harrison who labelled Concarneau 'Sardinopolis'.

But it was Harrison also who, with American directness, asked Bastien-Lepage about his technique, in particular whether he used the broad brush that was later to become the hallmark of the Newlyn school; until then, the older man had not used it, but forthwith did some studies using the broad brush. He commended Harrison for his paintings of the nude in the open air, and this naturally strengthened the American's reputation among younger artists such as Tuke. For his part, Harrison (though his own reputation declined) kept in contact with the British painters he met in France, and in 1899 stayed for a short period in St Ives.[10]

If Arthur Lemon had introduced Tuke to the pleasures of painting the nude under the Mediterranean sun, it was Harrison who showed him that painting the nude in the open air was not impractical in the colder climate of north-west Europe. As Tuke later wrote:

At the time I first took up the subject, when Alexander Harrison was attacking the same problem in the orchards of France, it seemed to open up fresh vistas, and certainly gave new interest to the study of the undraped figure.[11]

Harrison's work reflected Harry Tuke's instincts precisely. To see in the studio of Bastien-Lepage the sort of outdoor work in which he had delighted in Italy, and to be invited by the painter to bring something to show him, was to feel the reassurance of a kindred spirit.

A month later Tuke was back with his family in Bournemouth. He had been summoned home because his brother Willie's condition was worsening and his hold on life becoming tenuous. Happily, he rallied. Tuke used the waiting time to paint two small *plein air* pictures on the beach, using a friend and neighbour, May Hughes, daughter of the author of *Tom Brown's Schooldays*, Thomas Hughes, as model. He took the pictures back to Paris, and in mid-March was showing them to Bastien-Lepage.

> I expected he would just look at them and say 'pas mal'; not at all, he looked at each one and gave it me hot over most, which made me all the gladder when he said of my Bournemouth calm sea with pier, 'tres fin', and of others 'beaucoup de sentiment de couleur'. He liked Miss Hughes standing by the sea, and the panels of Canfino and Lorenzo [Italian boys], best. He said of most that they were only just begun, and that I ought to finish them to the last point possible. Sargent has also professed to be charmed with the calm sea.[12]

It was a bonus when one of the Bournemouth sketches, of May Hughes sitting on the beach, was accepted by the Royal Academy. In April, Tuke had time to spend a few days with Tom and Carrie Gotch who had rented a small house in the country outside Paris at Brolles, in preparation for the birth of their first child (a daughter, Phyllis, was born in September). He went for long walks with some of his student friends, in particular W. J. Wainwright from Birmingham, who was to become a distinguished water-colourist.

After a further month's work at the Laurens studio, Tuke returned to England, calling first on his family in Bournemouth and then travelling down to Torcross in South Devon. He had been persuaded by George Jacomb-Hood to spend a couple of months with him and his brothers in the fishing village that had become their summer home. Two other friends also joined them:

Benwell Clark and Chevallier Tayler. Jacomb-Hood and the others were content to put bathing, sailing and a little light sketching at the top of the holiday agenda, but Tuke, 'in his methodical and persevering way' as Jacomb-Hood put it,[13] no doubt inspired by his meeting with Bastien-Lepage, was determined to tackle a really big *plein air* painting. He wrote home:

> I am quite in love with the place, there are lots of charming things to be done, a great deal more than we can broach. The village people are extremely amiable and we are on the best of terms with nearly all. In consequence we have an inexhaustible supply of models. I have found a very beautiful spot, a boy sits asleep in an apple tree, in shadow, relieved by the village and sea in bright sunlight seen through the branches. A beautiful scene in reality but almost impossible to paint. The difficulties of coping with the monster canvas in the wind and sun are immense, though I am generally surrounded by a willing band of *gamins* ready to run for sticks or ropes as required. They also insist on using my paints, expensive ones preferred . . .[14]

The only discordant note was that Tayler and Clark would never get up at 6.30 or 7.00 when Tuke and Jacomb-Hood went out for their daily morning bathe and sail. It was on this holiday that Tuke learned to sail, his parents having been steadfastly against it during his Falmouth boyhood. When he first went out without a helpful fisherman Tuke told Jacomb-Hood that 'if his father and mother knew it they would have a fit'.[15] Sailing was soon to become one of his greatest passions.

Thus he began to reach toward the lifestyle that he was soon to adopt entirely. The morning bathe, the *plein air* painting, the afternoon sail, became his routine, and it was on this Torcross holiday that he found it. He discovered, too, the simple-hearted friendship and generosity of the fishermen and their sons, who would helpfully pose as models. He became particularly friendly with one fishing family, that of William Dimond, two of whose young sons sat for Tuke. Jack was then about seventeen, and Jim eleven. Jim Dimond was to reappear later in the artist's life. Tuke completed a portrait on panel of the father, one of Jack in the 'linney' (a covered drying-place for fishing gear), and a third one of the two sons on the beach. He also did two portraits of local worthies.[16]

But it was his big picture of the boy in the tree that preoccupied him. The local people became so familiar with it that it was known in Torcross as *Dally in the apple tree* (the boy model was Dally Hutchings, a village lad).[17] Returning to Paris with it in November, Tuke prepared to submit it to the Paris Salon, for which, no doubt correctly, he thought it better suited than for the Royal Academy of the day. He called it *Un Jour de Paresse* (A Lazy Day). Early in December he was asked to attend the first dinner of a club organised by John Singer Sargent. Tuke was to be one of the six members, and each was to bring a guest to the monthly dinner. On the following day Tuke took some of the members to see his picture, one of them Gustav Natorp, a German sculptor, friend of Henry James and Rodin's first pupil;[18] Tuke thought they 'seemed to be rather fetched by it', as he wrote to his mother:

> Most people think it at least very original, and advise me not to do too much to it, for fear of spoiling what I've got. I have made one important alteration, that is opening the eyes which nearly everyone recommended and I am sure it adds greatly to the interest . . . Sargent likes the one of Jack Dymond [sic] says it is the best thing I have painted, in which I agree with him.[19]

The big Torcross picture was indeed accepted and shown at the Salon.

His return to Paris involved Tuke in a number of pleasant but time-consuming visits to his father's medical contacts. He went down to Passy to have breakfast with Dr Blanche and his family; their artist son, Jacques-Emile, was moving to a new studio at Auteuil in the new year and invited Tuke to share it with him (at the reception to launch the studio Tuke was introduced to Oscar Wilde). With Jacomb-Hood, von Glehn and Millard he saw Sarah Bernhardt at the Vaudeville — 'magnificent'.[20] With such a busy social life he completed only two portraits. Both were of fellow-students. One, done in Tremblay's studio, was of Fred Millard; the other, at Laurens', of a French student, Horace Melicourt.

In March he once again crossed the Channel to spend a few days with his family at Bournemouth. Willie was still seriously ill; Harry painted a portrait of the local doctor's son in gratitude for Dr Falls' kindly care. Then, with commissions from Willie for particular postage stamps for their collection, he sailed for Cherbourg and walked the twelve miles to his friend Tremblay's home on the coast at Dielette. After a few days' holiday he set off for Paris. On the train he was handed a telegram: Willie was dying. Harry returned to cope with the family grief and help with the

11.   Study for *A Summer Morning*, oil, *c*.1886-88. R77 (Tuke Collection, Royal Cornwall Polytechnic Society).

12.   *On the Beach, Bournemouth*, oil, 1882. R10. (Private Collection).

funeral in Saffron Walden. On Willie's breast he put red camellias—that 'touch of red' that was to become familiar in so many paintings. To exacerbate his sorrows, he heard shortly afterwards that a picture he had submitted to the Royal Academy had been rejected.[21].

After his days in the Paris studio ended, he returned again for a few days in Normandy with Tremblay where he enjoyed 'the most gorgeous bathes in the morning off a jetty, dives up to any height from a flight of steps, into clear water like Cornish sea'.[22] Willie's death, coming at the end of his Paris student days, unsettled him. He was twenty-five. 'I have not made up my mind at all what to do yet, I am afraid of having rather a cut up summer', he wrote in June to Tom Gotch, the latter having gone down to Cornwall with his wife Carrie who was recovering from illness after the birth of their daughter. 'Is there much to do at Newlyn and who is down there? Millard and Todd for two, n'est ce pas'.[23] Ralph Todd, son of a wealthy man who had cut off his inheritance, shared Millard's studio.[24]

The decision was postponed while he went to Scotland with Jacomb-Hood to stay with James Paterson at Blairmore in Argyll, across the Clyde from Glasgow. He painted a portrait of Paterson (later President of the Royal Scottish Academy) but most of the holiday was spent sailing in all weathers. It was Tuke's first experience of a big boat, for Robert Paterson, James's elder brother, had a twenty-five-foot yacht, the *Louise*. 'We spent a rather stormy fortnight down and about the mouth of the Clyde, when . . . we never shook out a reef from our mainsail the whole time, except perhaps when we raced in the regatta at Largs'.[25] They came second, Tuke noted in his diary.

After Willie's death, Tuke's parents decided to move to Hanwell, in Middlesex, where Dr Tuke was to be a consultant at the asylum; he also took a consulting room in Welbeck Street, Mayfair, in the house of his future son-in-law, Dr Harrington Sainsbury. After his Scottish holiday Harry went down to Falmouth to help his parents sort out their stored possessions, then to move them up to Hanwell. If Falmouth aroused nostalgia, he had little time to indulge it. Once the family were settled into the new suburban house, he caught the train for the West Country, and Newlyn.

Newlyn was a fishing village a mile or so west of Penzance and ten miles from Land's End. It was on the western curve of Mount's Bay, and thus sheltered from the strong Atlantic winds. Most of its families relied on the sea for their livelihood, and while during the earlier years of the nineteenth century they had often faced poverty and privation, it happened that in the early 1880s there was a season of good catches and the Newlyn folk were, if not prospering, at least in no danger of starvation. As one of the Newlyn artists, Stanhope Forbes, wrote in 1884:

Never has there been such fishing known and were it not that fish are so cheap, the people would all be rolling in money. Boats are bringing in as many as 12,000 mackerel and the great difficulty is to find means of packing these large quantities.[26]

Evidently Tuke chose Newlyn because Tom and Carrie Gotch were there, as were other friends from the Slade and from Paris, notably Fred Millard and William Wainwright. The latter had no doubt been attracted to Newlyn because it was popular with his Birmingham friends, particularly Walter Langley, newly-elected to the Royal Institute of Painters in Watercolour, and acknowledged among his peers, as Tuke called him, 'the strongest watercolour man in England'. There was also Edwin Harris, another Birmingham artist, who had studied in Antwerp with Wainwright. A few of the artists had the means to rent houses; others took rooms with local people who were to be their models.

Tuke found himself a room with a view across the bay, in the house on Trewarveneth Street of a local boat-builder, Philip Harvey, who, with his family, soon became a good friend. Tuke commissioned a sailing boat from him, and also a model of it. In the three months that Tuke spent in Newlyn on this visit, he made numerous sketches but painted comparatively little. Apart from small portraits of Philip Harvey and his younger brother Tom, he completed two pictures in the tackle cellar under the house. One, which he called *Ship Builders*, was of a youngster making a model schooner, watched by a little girl. The second, *Dinner Time*, was of a scruffy small boy in a cap, interrupted in his lunch in the sail store. The small boy had the remarkable name of Ambrose Rouffignac.

If you got so grand as to keep a tiger [groom], he would do very well, he is very paintable and has a nice Cornish accent.[27]

Ship Builders was sent up to London and shown at the first exhibition of the Nineteenth Century Art Society in Conduit Street. The Society had been started by R. S. Marriott and W. G. Freeman to show the work of younger artists who, many felt, were not being fairly treated by a reactionary Royal Academy (no unfamiliar criticism in any generation). Tuke's painting was favourably noticed in the *Standard*, and bought for 50 guineas, less 10 percent discount, by a leading dealer, C. W. Dowdeswell. It was the beginning of a profitable association.

Tuke was drawn away from Newlyn in November by family duties, first to paint a portrait of Dr Falls, his brother's doctor, in Bournemouth, and then a small portrait—done from a photograph—of his Saffron Walden uncle, George Gibson, who had recently died. He also embarked upon a major portrait of his sister Maria, now twenty-two and herself a budding artist, who was very willing to sit as a model for her much-loved brother. He posed her in an ornately carved chair specially bought for the purpose, wearing a black satin dress with delicate white lace at the throat and cuffs, against a green plush background. Her hair is drawn back, and the eyes shine brilliantly out of the picture. It was a considerable success at the Royal Academy of 1884.

Dowdeswell, the dealer, also commissioned his own portrait from Tuke. Whistler admired it, and invited Tuke to his studio. That spring Dowdeswell obtained several lucrative portrait commissions for him: a County Court judge (Frank Bacon), a leading printer (Philip Waterlow), and a publisher (F. S. Ellis, publisher

of William Morris). With each of these, Tuke was obliged to cope with the time pressures of men of the world, who would only fit in an hour or so for sittings early in the morning. His reputation as an efficient and competent craftsman, unself-conscious, a pleasant conversationalist and a good listener, able to get on with people from all ranks of society, was made. After Dowdeswell's commission he netted £50 8s 0d for such a portrait.

At the end of May 1884 he was on the train back to Newlyn, lodging again with the Harvey family. This time he was able to do some paintings in the open air. One was of Philip Harvey with his daughter, Janie. Tuke recorded that while they 'sat and stood' for the picture, Janie's head was 'afterwards done *de chic*'[28]—the first time he adopted what was to become a habit, interchanging heads and bodies for artistic effect. Another depicted Sarah Ann Stevenson, the little girl from *Ship Builders*, in Walter Langley's orchard. He then began a picture using two local boys as models. He posed them in Philip Harvey's punt *Little Argo*, one stripped to the waist, the other in a smock and hat, both hands on a sculling oar. The two boys were John Wesley Kitching and John Rouffignac Cotton. The picture caused great amusement among the quay lads, who would follow Tuke with cries of 'There's John Wesley all

13. *Summer-time*, oil, 1884. R44.
(present whereabouts unknown).

14. Portrait of James Paterson, oil, 1883. (Private Collection).

naked!'.[29] Entitled *Summer-time*, the picture was shown at the Grosvenor Gallery later that year and bought by Dowdeswell for £80: four years later it was re-sold for £110. This was the first of Tuke's 'boys and boats' pictures.

In July he spent a week or two on a yacht chartered by the painter William Ayerst Ingram, who was based at St Ives. Ingram had made a reputation as a marine artist; his expertise in painting the sea and shipping, gained not least during voyages to Australia, no doubt endeared him to Tuke. It seems probable that Jacomb-Hood made the introduction, and was also on board, for he recalled that 'my friend Ayerst Ingram . . . chartered a small yacht with a crew of two men and a boy, for the purpose of doing a series of water-colours of sea and ports on the South coast from the Needles to Falmouth. With him I spent a month or more cruising, very often at night, while we anchored and painted during the day'. It was on the *Verbena* in Falmouth that Tuke sketched what he called *A Bit of Falmo' Harbour*, noting: 'My first pastel finished'.[30] He sold it for 5 guineas.

Perhaps it was on that visit to Falmouth by sea that Harry Tuke began seriously to consider living there again. He had made many friends in Newlyn, and many more were arriving (at one time in the early 1880s it was said that there were twenty-seven artists in residence, so that the local people would say to any artist: 'Do 'ee want me to set for 'ee?').[31] But his closest friends had moved out: the Gotches had gone to Australia and on their return were settling in Hampstead (though they returned to Newlyn later). Chevallier Tayler was also leaving Newlyn that winter. There was also the fact that the artists' colony in Newlyn was becoming 'organised', not least by Stanhope Forbes who was to become the focus of the Newlyn school, particularly after his marriage (slightly to the irritation of some of the earlier ex-Birmingham residents).[32] The Forbeses became great organisers of social occasions: amateur concerts, cricket matches. Tuke was gregarious and loved cricket, but he was in Newlyn to paint.

Back at his parents' home in Hanwell for Christmas, Tuke led a busy social life, going for country walks, to the theatre and concerts, playing bridge, and visiting the Gotches at Hampstead, conveniently close to the studio he had rented in King Henry's Road for the winter. There he completed a large formal portrait of his deceased uncle George Gibson, a commission from the Borough of Saffron Walden (where Gibson had been Mayor). He was paid 100 guineas for it.

The Royal Academy had accepted two of his pictures: the Dowdeswell portrait, and a costume picture, *Before the Rehearsal*, of two young girls who were neighbours at Hanwell, but both works were 'skied' (hung too high for good viewing). It can have been little consolation that many of his Newlyn friends had their work rejected, though a sketch of Falmouth harbour by his sister Maria, an amateur, was well hung. The great success of the Academy that year was a large picture, five-and-a-half feet by nine, *A Fish Sale on a Cornish Beach*. The beach was Newlyn and the artist Stanhope Forbes.[33]

1 Artists' Letters: Henry Scott Tuke to T. C. Gotch, 12 March 1881, No.128
2 Maria Tuke Sainsbury, p.55
3 G. P. Jacomb-Hood: *With Brush and Pencil*, Murray 1925, p.16
4 G. P. Jacomb-Hood, *op. cit.*, p.21
5 Maria Tuke Sainsbury, p.57
6 G. P. Jacomb-Hood, *op. cit.*, p.21
7 Maria Tuke Sainsbury, p.59
8 *ibid*
9 Stanhope Forbes: 'Cornwall from a Painter's Point of View', reprinted from the *Annual Report of the Royal Cornwall Polytechnic Society for 1900*, Falmouth 1901, p.7
10 Michael Jacobs, *The Good and Simple Life: Artist Colonies in Europe and America*, Phaidon, 1985, p.148
11 Charles Kains Jackson, 'Henry Scott Tuke, ARA', *The Magazine of Art*, 1903, p.338
12 Maria Tuke Sainsbury, p.60
13 G. P. Jacomb-Hood, p.26
14 Maria Tuke Sainsbury, p.62
15 G. P. Jacomb-Hood, p.26
16 Henry Scott Tuke Registers (R13 and R17)
17 G. P. Jacomb Hood, p.26
18 Stanley Olson: *John Singer Sargent*, Macmillan 1986, pp.181-2
19 Artists' Letters: Henry Scott Tuke to E. M. Tuke, 10 Dec 1882, No.156
20 Maria Tuke Sainsbury, pp.63-4
21 Maria Tuke Sainsbury, p.66
22 Artists' Letters: Henry Scott Tuke to T. C. Gotch, 9 June 1883, No.157
23 *ibid*
24 C. Fox and F. Greenacre, *op. cit.*, p.67
25 G. P. Jacomb-Hood, p.318
26 Stanhope Forbes, quoted in Fox and Greenacre, *op. cit.*, p.32
27 Maria Tuke Sainsbury, p.70
28 Henry Scott Tuke Registers (R36)
29 Henry Scott Tuke Registers (R44): Kitching's story was tragic. HST records in this Register entry that he 'was killed or drowned at Cowes in the Autumn of 1905 and one of his shipmates was tried for murder but acquitted—another shipmate who was concerned hung himself on the yacht'.
30 Henry Scott Tuke Registers (R38)
31 Fox and Greenacre, *op. cit.*, p.35
32 Fox and Greenacre, *op. cit.*, pp.51-4
33 Maria Tuke Sainsbury, p.75

15.   Tuke in a dinghy at Falmouth, *c.*1901. From Lamorna Birch's photograph album. (Private Collection).

CHAPTER THREE
Coming Home

By May 1885 Harry Tuke had made up his mind. He took the train down to Falmouth, and walked out to Sunny Cove between Swanpool and Pennance Point. There was a house on the cliffs, above the beach, looking out across Falmouth Bay, crowded with shipping, to the lighthouse. The place was owned by the Fox family, who were friends of his. It was occupied by two women and their families. He asked if they would rent two rooms to him. They agreed: 'Jolly rooms tho' bare, looking on the bay'.[1] Settling up with the women, he returned to London to make plans for the summer; and that included finding a boy model.

The model Tuke chose was a Cockney lad, Walter Shilling, who was already modelling on a regular basis for life classes at the Slade. Tuke delayed his departure for about a month in order to finish one portrait of *F. S. Ellis* in Torquay, begun in London the previous year, and to carry out, at one sitting 'save a few touches next day',[2] another of *R. S. Marriott*, a picture dealer who was also one of the administrators of the Nineteenth Century Art Society in Conduit Street. This may have been the portrait for which Tuke later recalled having to resort to desperate measures when the sitter became overheated:

> Various remedies were tried, in order to modify his complexion and temperature, but all to no purpose. In the end we had recourse to the cold tap, which I turned on his head at intervals, till seven o'clock in the evening, when the portrait was finished.[3]

By 7 June 1885 Tuke was ready to leave London and that evening he and Shilling boarded the mail train at Paddington. The thick sea-mist which greeted them on arrival at Falmouth the following morning soon lifted, and Tuke wrote enthusiastically of his new home:

> We have the most exquisite imaginable of views, looking out to sea and to the Castle [Pendennis], a dead calm with gleaming sun most of the day.[4]

Immediately below the cliffs on which Pennance Cottage stood was a beach where Tuke bathed (a daily habit when in Falmouth, as there was no water supply in the cottage) and where he soon installed a small boat. Next to this was Sunny

Cove, where Tuke had learned to swim as a child, and around Pennance (or 'Stack')[5] Point was another beach—much wider than Sunny Cove—which faced away from the town towards Rosemullion Head and the Manacles to the south. Tuke was quick to recognise the possibilities for his work offered by this place, for, he declared after a few weeks:

> Newporth Beach is the principal seat of operations, it is a truly enchanted spot.[6]

Unchanged and even now little visited, Sunny Cove and Newporth Beach still retain the qualities which Tuke found so irresistible, providing him with enough visual inspiration to last a lifetime. The beaches were inaccessible enough to be out of sight to all but the most curious, being reached in each case by scrambling down precipitous and overgrown paths. Newporth Beach in particular was more easily reached by boat, and the sight of Tuke being rowed around the headland at the end of the day's work, the canvas held firmly across the praam (flat-bottomed boat) like a large sail, left a lasting memory with those who witnessed it.

Unlike Sunny Cove, which is a smooth sandy beach enclosed by two rocky arms, Newporth Beach—a mixture of sand and shingle—is reefed with rocks running all the way along the water's

16. Photograph of Tuke taken by Arthur Tanner, 1885. (Private Collection).

edge, creating rock pools and gullies which provided an infinite variety of settings for Tuke's paintings. The chief beauty of both beaches however lies in the shallowness of the water as it shelves gradually beyond the rocks, revealing the sea bed through a translucent film of blues and greens ranging from pale turquoise to deep ultramarine, colours faithfully reproduced in Tuke's paintings. Other artists have returned obsessively to a single theme and found something new to say in each fresh interpretation, but few have recorded their chosen spot as lovingly as Tuke or with so much individuality — in many paintings it is possible to identify the exact part of the beach on which they were painted.

For the first month, Tuke found it difficult to settle, and to decide how he should proceed. He completed a small watercolour which he called, appropriately, *Coming Home*; its subject was Shilling walking through a meadow above the cottage, a fisherman's net over his shoulder. Eventually Tuke planned the summer's output; he decided to concentrate on

> a great bathing picture . . . , 3 principal figures and two small. I have another little fishing one for grey days, and a lying down afternoon sunny one. There is a great saving of time in having the same model and being able to work all pretty near together.[7]

The Bathers, depicting nude boys on the rocks at Newporth Beach, was an ambitious undertaking and marked his first serious attempt at painting the nude in the open air since his Italian experiments. Walter Shilling was the model not only for the two fisher boys and the reclining figure on the beach, but also for all the figures in *The Bathers*. 'I am almost tired of painting the same boy' said Tuke, who was also becoming rather irritated by Shilling's cheeky Cockneyisms, 'but in the bathing picture I consider him quite impersonal, the vehicle of splendid flesh colour and form'.[8] It was not an easy job for the young model, for as Tuke told an interviewer some years later, 'When I first began painting nudes out of doors the model sat out till mid-November, and I used to watch him going pink and blue in patches'.[9]

The three beach pictures were completed by the autumn, when Shilling went home to Kentish Town. Early in 1886 Tuke was one of a group of young painters, most of whom had studied in Paris,[10] who were instrumental in the formation of the New English Art Club, in conscious opposition to what they saw as the insularity of home-produced art, particularly that which found most favour at the Royal Academy. Their leader was the painter W. H. Bartlett whose father, John Bartlett, was a London dealer and friend of Martin Colnaghi, who had just taken over the Marlborough Gallery in Pall Mall. The latter offered it free of charge to the group of young painters for an exhibition in April 1886.

The group met urgently in London on 4 January 1886, and constituted themselves as the New English Art Club. Their Chairman was W. J. Laidley, and among the participants, with Tuke, were several of his friends including Gotch and Jacomb-Hood and other Newlyn artists, among them Stanhope Forbes. The list of Tuke's

17. William Martin: *The Cottage at Pennance*, watercolour, *c*.1930. (Private Collection).

18.   *A Morning Gossip*, oil, 1885. R58. (Collection John R. Heckenlively, MD).

fellow exhibitors also included two, John Singer Sargent and Philip Wilson Steer, who were soon to become amongst the most highly-regarded painters of their generation, and it is an indication of the real conservatism of British art at that time that they, as well as Henry Herbert la Thangue, Frank Bramley,[11] Stanhope Forbes and several of the other Newlyn artists, could ever have been regarded as truly avant-garde.

However, after Colnaghi had seen the paintings submitted, 'particularly one of nude boys', he withdrew his support. The painting to which he so strongly objected was evidently Tuke's *The Bathers*.[12] W. J. Laidley personally guaranteed the rent of the gallery for two years, and the show went ahead, opening on 12 April.[13]

Soon after his return to Falmouth, Tuke had done two portraits for local friends, *Alfred Lloyd Fox*, a portrait for his widow, and *Charlie Genn*, son of Falmouth's Town Clerk. He also painted Mrs Andrews and Mrs Fouracre, his landladies, the latter with her little son, Richard. Then Tuke visited his old friends at Newlyn. Stanhope Forbes wrote after his visit that Tuke

likes the place [Falmouth] very much but can get no models and has been forced to have a boy from London whom he boards and lodges. So he is painting this British youth in the style the British matron so strongly objects to. Later he will return to Newlyn.[14]

Stanhope Forbes' confident prediction was wrong. Although the circumstances for Tuke's painting were not yet ideal and the shortage of models was a serious problem, there was still much to hold him to Falmouth, not least the many friends he and his family had made during their residence there, and the town itself which had seen great developments since his childhood. Falmouth in 1885 was a thriving little port of about 10,000 inhabitants, having largely recovered from its mid-century slump caused by the decline in the Packet Service. As sail began to give way to steam, and internal communications (notably the railway) improved, the Packet Service declined, and its transference to Southampton in 1850 caused serious hardship and unemployment in Falmouth.

In 1860 the foundation stone was laid in Falmouth for the building of dry docks, originally conceived in a vain attempt to attract the Packet Service back to Falmouth. By the 1880s, now concentrating on ship repair and small-scale ship construction, the docks were solidly prosperous — their workforce soon to be the provider of several of Tuke's models. The extension of the railway to Falmouth (the branch line from Truro opened in 1863), which enabled many more visitors to reach the town, was another outward sign of the mood of renewed optimism and modest wellbeing in Falmouth.[15] By the time Tuke settled there, the town was being confidently marketed as a watering-place with unrivalled health-giving properties.[16]

Most importantly for Tuke, sailing for pleasure had become a popular sport in Falmouth, encouraged by the formation there of the Royal Cornwall Yacht Club, in 1872.[17] Falmouth's large natural harbour provided a safe haven for small craft from all but the most violent easterly gales, and its reputation as one of the finest sailing resorts in the south-west has been maintained to this day. Tuke was glad to find a kindred spirit in John Henry Eva Downing, son of old family friends (his father had a ship chandler's business on the harbour), in whose yacht *Shadow* they sailed to Plymouth to take part in races there. 'I find Downing much the most energetic and therefore congenial companion here'.[18] Tuke had already ordered a sailing boat — the *Cornish Girl* — to be built for him by Philip Harvey in Newlyn, and after wintering as usual in Saffron Walden and London, he was keen to rush back to Falmouth and try out another new vessel, the *Lily*. She was a 'quay punt' — nothing like the punts of the Isis or Cam, but a fast sailing boat with a deep forefoot, of a type used mainly for carrying messages to vessels within the inner harbour.

Within a few days of his return, Tuke made another discovery which was to prove invaluable: new boats always attracted the attention of the youngsters who thronged the harbour. One of those harbour boys was Jack Rowling, then sixteen years old. At first Tuke described him as a 'quay scamp'. 'Got hold of Jack Rowling and stuck him up in the Lily. He promises to be a treasure'.[19] Tuke was beginning the first of many portraits of him, a small oil, *Our Jack*. It was also Tuke's first major picture painted on board ship. This portrait was given to Tom and Carrie Gotch as a belated wedding present. Jack Rowling (or Rolling — the spelling varies) was described by Tuke's sister Maria, who met him, as 'a very lovable young barbarian who could look like an angel and behave like a demon'.[20] His lack of self-consciousness when being painted made him a natural model, and moreover, as befitted one who had grown up by water, he looked entirely at home in a boat. It is significant that of the twenty works recorded by Tuke in his Registers during the next year, thirteen are of Jack. All but two are clothed; the one 'bathing' picture has Jack in white trousers and hat, though stripped to the waist. For seven years Tuke scarcely visited Newporth Beach except to swim, and painted few male nudes.

In June 1886 Tuke added to his steadily expanding little fleet of vessels with the purchase of an old French brigantine, the *Julie of Nantes*, which had been condemned as unseaworthy and offered for sale in Falmouth harbour by the French Admiralty, her previous owners. 'Downing and Lean bid for me, she only fetched £41',[21] (by coincidence, almost exactly the sum he was paid for the sale of *Two Falmouth Fisherboys* around the same time). The *Julie* was moored off Greenbank and her leaks plugged sufficiently to make it safe for her to undertake short coastal trips. Tuke and his friends stripped her out, cleared the hold to give Tuke a studio sixty feet long, but the upper deck with its masts and rigging was left intact. The elements of primitive living—a stove, a table, some crockery and cutlery, and hammocks—were installed. They slept on board for the first time on 20 July 1886: Tuke, John Downing, Arthur Tanner and Jim Dimond. Tanner had been a school friend of Tuke's at Weston-super-Mare, had travelled abroad with him on a youthful holiday, and also became an artist: he is recorded as a landscape painter, living in Lamorna and 'friendly with Lamorna Birch and Tuke'.[22] He was a bachelor, and it is said he had a private income which, paid quarterly, enabled him to spend lavishly for short periods and then retire abroad until his next cheque was due. Until his death in 1915 he remained one of Tuke's closest friends, stayed frequently with him at Swanpool, was a kindly critic of his work and shared many of his pleasures—bathing, sailing, and (later) cycling. Jim Dimond (brother of Jack) had met Tuke during his holiday at Torcross with Jacomb-Hood a year or two earlier; and, as a keen and skilful young sailor, was a useful addition to this first crew.

The purchase of the *Julie* came at a providential time for Tuke; although he maintained that his studio was 'out of doors', he was clearly hampered by the lack of adequate storage space at the cottage, and by having nowhere to carry out the increasing number of portrait commissions that were beginning to come his way. After a few weeks the vessel began to serve as a second home. The two families who were occupying the cottage at Pennance when Tuke first lived there had fallen out among themselves and left. The family which followed them—the Jewells—turned out to be so disagreeable[23] that Tuke, who could not bear to live in an uncongenial atmosphere, preferred to stay on board the *Julie* rather than go home to constant rows. The Jewells in their turn moved out the following spring and were replaced by one of the original families to have lived there, the Fouracres; but although this was a more satisfactory arrangement, Tuke was by then so

19. Jack Rowling (left), Tuke and Jim Dimond on the *Julie of Nantes*, c.1885. (Private Collection).

21. *The Promise*, oil, 1887. R92. (Courtesy of the National Museums and Galleries on Merseyside, Walker Art Gallery).

Facing page: 20. *Our Jack*, oil, 1886. R62. (Tuke Collection, RCPS).

22.   *Land in Sight*, oil, 1887-88. R93. (present whereabouts unknown).

enjoying the freedom of his new way of life and the romance of living on the water that he remained on the *Julie* for the best part of three years.

Tuke's was not the only floating studio in Falmouth harbour at that time—the marine artist Charles Napier Hemy, who had moved to Cornwall four years before Tuke, owned a converted Seine barge, and subsequently a much more luxurious vessel, the *Vandermeer*, purpose-built on the keel and hull of a yacht, in which Hemy could spend several days at sea with a small crew.[24] Hemy was seventeen years older than Tuke, an aloof and rather forbidding figure whose fierce eyes above a hawk-like nose betrayed a hint of fanaticism. Nevertheless the two men maintained a firm friendship for over thirty years—reportedly surviving a certain coolness on one occasion when Tuke had the temerity to criticise one of Hemy's paintings[25]—despite the fact that they held different views on almost every subject from religion to art (Hemy was a devout Catholic, who had spent a period as a Dominican monk). Both were generous in their appreciation of each other's work and after his election to Associate Membership of the Royal Academy, Hemy wrote in reply to Tuke's congratulatory note:

> I thought . . . that they had given up all idea of making me an A.R.A. . . . . *You* were the next I thought, and you ought to be . . . You are far too good, and . . . too sincere an artist to be outside.[26]

Their working methods were also quite different. Hemy rarely painted in the open air and his floating studio was used only to make drawings and sketches which would be worked into the finished painting in his studio on dry land; through his careful planning and at times meticulous attention to detail, he revealed the debt he owed to the Pre-Raphaelite painters he had admired so much in his early twenties.[27]

The *Julie* was an exceptionally picturesque sight even in the days when sailing vessels of all sizes thronged the harbour. Stanhope Forbes visited him on board in 1887:

> Tuke showed us his pictures which are simply beautiful. Gave us a wonderful tea under stranger conditions than ever I took that meal before. It is a strange life to lead and only a man like Tuke could do it, but it suits him exactly, and he had subjects all round him such as he likes to paint best of all. We left him at last delighted with his ship and his work.[28]

During this period, Tuke did indeed find plenty of subject matter on the *Julie* and the surrounding vessels in the inner harbour. Jack Rowling, who joined him in living on board for much of the time, was his principal model, cast in various roles from ship's cook to deckhand according to the requirements of the painting. One painting of Jack was completed on shore: it was painted in the orchard above the cottage (and so echoed the successful orchard picture painted at Torcross during Tuke's student days) and is called *The Promise*. It portrays Jack in fisherman's jersey and cap, as youthful lover, holding the hand of a young girl (described by Tuke in his Register as 'his sweetheart's sister, Jessie Nicholls from Flushing'). It is a touching picture, and could signify Tuke's acceptance that Jack's affections were directed towards girls. However, Jack had become Tuke's particular care, as well as his racing companion, and constant model.

Of the other visitors to the *Julie*, Walter Shilling came down again from London in 1887. Possibly this second visit was at Shilling's own instigation, or perhaps he had been sent for because Jack, who had become a diver, was working elsewhere. At any rate he appeared in only one small oil (*Foc's'l Companions*) and three watercolours, none of which were bathing scenes, before he reputedly started to suffer from fits and was hastily despatched back to London. Mrs Shilling wrote to Tuke in gratitude for his kindness, attributing her son's fits to 'constant exercise in the pure sea air, causing him to eat too much of much superior food [than] that to which he had been used, thus making his blood too thick'. Walter himself wrote later, an engaging letter signed 'Walter 1/-' and full of messages to his friends in Falmouth and

23. Jack Rowling sculling near the *Julie*, Falmouth, c.1885. (Private Collection).

25.   Portrait of Lucy Genn, oil, 1885. (Falmouth School).

Facing page: 24.   *All Hands to the Pumps!*, oil, 1889. R118. (National Maritime Museum, London).

requests for photographs of 'the tea treat at Helford River',[29] but he never modelled for Tuke again and their acquaintance appears to have come to an end.

Tuke's father had come to Falmouth for a visit within a few weeks of his son moving there, and later his mother and sister, with her friend Rosa Marriage, spent two summers (1887 and 1888) in rooms overlooking the harbour. Perhaps each of them had been a little apprehensive at first in case the unconventional course taken by the quietly determined Harry had not succeeded. They need not have worried: 'We fully realised what a delightful life Harry was leading, healthy for both mind and body'.[30] Tuke was beginning to prosper in Falmouth; already members of the influential Fox family, and the Genns who had been near neighbours of the Tukes in Woodlane, had loyally commissioned portraits, several of which were actually painted on the *Julie*. And in 1887 Tuke was the artist chosen by the Town Council to paint the presentation portrait of *William Genn*, celebrating his fifty years' service as Town Clerk.

More importantly his work was starting to receive official recognition in London. The paintings accepted for exhibition at the Royal Academy between 1887 and 1891 had all except one been painted on the *Julie*, and all had, in the Newlyn tradition, strong anecdotal content with titles like *Land in Sight*, *A Sailor's Yarn*, *Try my Soup*, and *Euchre* (the last a popular card game among the men of the Falmouth waterfront).[31] It was the painting exhibited in 1889 which brought Tuke his first major success.

I am just ordering a stretcher for my great pumping picture [Tuke wrote in the previous September]. [It] is to be rather a big venture, about ten figures altogether . . . all this is quite contrary to your notions of my doing small pictures, but I am rather of Mr Bartlett's opinion that 'the big uns get yer name up, Tooke'.[32]

'Mr Bartlett' was presumably John Bartlett, the London picture dealer involved with the start of the New English Art Club; and *All Hands to the Pumps*, as the painting was called, certainly achieved its object in getting Tuke's 'name up'. It was hung on the line at the Royal Academy and bought from there in May by the Chantrey Fund for the South Kensington Museum (and thence to the Tate Gallery when it was opened in 1897) for £420, four times as much as Tuke had earned from the sale of any previous picture. A well-planned arrangement of seven figures (whittled down from the ten originally planned), the models were

Falmouth fishermen: Neddy Hall, Sam Hingston, William Hodge, Jimmy Nicholls and Denny Morrison; and there was also a windswept and instantly recognisable Jack Rowling clinging monkey-like to the rigging. The picture was described as 'if not the best storm at sea ever painted . . . very near to unique, in its incidents being possible and its dangers unexaggerated'.[33] If the composition now appears a little contrived to modern eyes, it should be remembered that alongside more typical fare to which the seasoned art-goer was accustomed—the huge and sprawling neo-classical friezes by Lord Leighton and Tuke's old professor at the Slade, Sir Edward Poynter, historical and modern costume-pieces by James Tissot and W. F. Yeames,[34] and sentimental rural idylls by Miles Birket Foster and Albert Goodwin—Tuke's contemporary realism was a refreshing change.

26. *A Sailor's Yarn*, oil, 1887. R78. The models are Jack Rowling, Dolphy Jewell and John Downing. (Collection of the Art Gallery of New South Wales).

Above: 27.   Jack Rowling.
(Private Collection).

Above right: 28.   Tuke with
Jack Rowling, c.1886.
(Private Collection).

Not everyone liked it. Tuke himself told how he was in the gallery when he found a policeman and some other men standing in front of it.

'Well, I'm blessed if I can see anything in it', said one. 'No, indeed,' the policeman corroborated. 'It's just a fake up. 'E's got a few dock-hands and put 'em together; but I guess 'e don't know no more about a ship than I do!'[35]

The anecdote, and Tuke's pleasure in it, demonstrates not only his sense of humour, but also his ingrained belief in the need for visual accuracy and truth in painting, recognised or not. The success of this picture formed part of a double family celebration; for it was completed in time for Tuke to attend the wedding in London of his sister Maria to Dr Harrington Sainsbury. He had been a Court Physician at Windsor and (appealingly to Tuke) had sailed round the world. Following the Chantrey success, Tuke post-

poned his intended departure for Falmouth and with some of his new-found wealth treated himself to a trip to Paris. He was accompanied by Cecil Castle, the fourteen-year-old cousin and lifelong companion of a new friend, Charles Kains Jackson, a London solicitor who was also the editor from 1888 to 1894 of the art magazine *The Artist and Journal of Home Culture*.[36] In Paris, as well as visiting the Salon, Tuke re-acquainted himself with the paintings of Bastien-Lepage, which he still greatly admired: '*Jeanne d'Arc* far, far and away the finest thing here to my fancy . . . Also *Les Foins* . . . very fine'.[37] Seeing the painting again a few years later, Tuke confirmed his admiration of *Les Foins* (*The Haymakers*),

one of the few pictures which makes a thrill run up my back, which according to Havelock Ellis is religion.[38]

Bastien-Lepage had died five years before, but was still mourned by his followers in Cornwall. Tuke's next major subject-picture was a good example of the subdued grey-brown tonalities and the theme of semi-rural simplicity beloved by Bastien-Lepage, even if the handling was considerably more fluid than his mentor would have advised. Painted between April and November 1890 in the kitchen of Tuke's cottage—domestic harmony having been restored—*The Message* featured his housekeeper Mrs Fouracre with her two young sons Georgie and Richard, and framed

29.   *The Fisherman* (also known as *Whiffing*), oil, 1888. R119. (Nottingham Castle Museum and Art Gallery).

in the doorway a new model, William J. Martin, who was in real life, as he appeared in this painting, a Post Office messenger boy.

William Martin also appeared that winter in *The Lamp Cleaners*, the last important painting to be done on board the *Julie*, which was showing signs of further decay, this time irreparable. The 'Great Blizzard'[39] in March 1891, in which Tuke lost three of his smaller vessels, including the

30. Tuke painting *The Fisherman* (see fig. 29). (Private Collection).

Cornish Girl and his quay punt *Lily*, was the beginning of the end: 'The good old *Julie* held on magnificently, but a lot of water in her; had her pumped out',[40] and Tuke's last spring aboard her was marred by an acute attack of boils, which caused him to miss Varnishing Day and the Private View of that year's Academy. A fellow artist (could it have been Stanhope Forbes?) made snide implications about the cause of the boils, which Tuke treated with righteous indignation. 'I like the idea of anyone from Newlyn making strictures on the air of the *Julie*. There could not be a more bogus idea'.[41] Nevertheless the *Julie*'s days were clearly numbered, and it was with deep regret the following year that Tuke finally relinquished her into the hands of a boat-yard owner to languish on the shores of the Penryn river until she finally disintegrated altogether.

The demise of the *Julie* brought with it the gradual fading from the scene of Jack Rowling, the model who more than any other had been so much part of Tuke's life aboard the vessel and for whom he always retained a special affection. Jack's work as a diver increasingly took him far from Cornwall, something he tried hard at first to resist. A rather incoherent and obviously very

homesick note to Tuke from London in January 1890 begged the artist to use his influence to help him find work nearer to home:

> My dear Sir
>
> You are very dear to me, I shall never be able to do enough for you . . . I don't like it up here . . . Would you write a letter to make things right for me to go home . . . I will make up the money to you in evening sittings when I get back.
>
> I hope you will be better soon. I want to go back with you, if you can't arrange it I will send home for some money for my fare, I am not going to stop in London another week.
>
> Goodbye my dear, God bless you. XXXXXXXX

In Tuke's writing at the end of the note is: 'From Jack Rowling'.[42]

Jack evidently became resigned in the end to travelling, for his outstanding ability to stay down for long spells in very deep water meant that he was much in demand for salvage operations from wrecked ships all round the coast of England and abroad. Wrecks were always dramatic events and in the days before newspaper photography became commonplace, artists could make money by producing eye-witness sketches for the illustrated papers. Tuke witnessed several wrecks off the treacherous Cornish coast. Two of them actively involved Jack, whose first experience of a major disaster was the loss of the *Bay of Panama* off Porthallow, in which eighteen people perished. A sketch Tuke made of the vessel, a four-masted steel ship which was the largest of the many victims of the Great Blizzard of 1891, was sold to the *Illustrated London News*. Seven years later, the 8000-ton steamer *Mohegan* ran on to the Manacles, only about fifty being saved out of a hundred and eighty passengers and crew:

> She seems to have been entirely out of her course as the weather was clear and it was only just dark . . . went down in a steamer to sketch yesterday morning, but there was not much to see, only the four masts and funnel just showing.[43] I am going to do a little drawing on the chance of the Daily Graphic taking it.[44]

A few days later, Tuke wrote

> Today we have been down with the salvage party to the wrecked steamer and seen the diving going on. I think I told you that Jack Rowling had been sent down by the Liverpool

Facing page: 31. *Perseus and Andromeda*, oil, 1889. R121.
(present whereabouts unknown).

Salvage Company for whom he works, to dive for the cargo, so we went down with him. He is now a very expert hand at the work, and earns anything between two and ten pounds a week. He was down in 60 feet of water once for an hour and a half, and a second time about an hour, and in that time sent up 66 pigs of tin, worth £264; very fascinating to watch real treasures of the deep coming up.[45]

Jack Rowling reached the height of his profession, his most distinguished feat being the salvage, in a dangerous current, of £200,000 worth of rubber from a sunken ship in the River Amazon, but the arduous conditions of diving ruined his health, causing his early death at the age of forty-nine.[46]

It is curious that Tuke never painted Jack nude, although his elder brother Willy appeared incongruously as the unfortunate maiden in Tuke's version of *Perseus and Andromeda*, shown at the Academy in 1890 to a mixed reception. The

painting was one of only four 'bathing' subjects he produced in the five years since those for which Walter Shilling had modelled that first summer in Falmouth. Two were illustrations of classical stories, including a large pastel of *Leander*[47]— 'One that I own I should be willing to stake my reputation on'[48]—which was shown at the Grosvenor Gallery in the same year that Tuke served on the hanging committee with George Clausen and William Stott of Oldham. That Tuke apparently felt it necessary to justify those of his paintings of the nude which were intended for exhibition by giving them the respectability of classical contexts may have been a consequence of the Colnaghi episode; in any event, although these works did have their admirers,[49] most observers seemed to feel that the putative Greek heroes portrayed were all too obviously Cornish fisherlads forced into uncomfortably artificial roles. Through a common friend (Horatio Brown) a correspondence began around this time between Tuke and the writer John Addington Symonds, and although the friendship was short-lived (Symonds died in 1893), he offered the painter some sound advice on the matter:

> I should say you ought to develop studies in the nude without pretending to make them 'subject pictures' . . . Your own inspiration is derived from nature's beauty. Classical or Romantic mythologies are not your starting point. Number your pictures Op.1, 2, 3 etc. Do not find titles for them. Let them go forth as transcripts from the beauty of the world. It won't pay? No, I suppose it won't.[50]

An old friend from student days at the Slade, Walter Dalrymple, now Sir Walter Hamilton-Dalrymple Bart., invited Tuke to Scotland in 1891 to do portraits of his mother, wife and daughter. The commission was worth £100 for the three pictures, and Tuke accepted. First he travelled north to Moniaive for a brief August holiday with his friend James Paterson and his wife, and then went down to Dalrymple's house at Leuchie, North Berwick, on the coast east of Edinburgh. The portraits eventually turned out well. While in Scotland he was commissioned to paint portraits of the six children of John Parrott of San Mateo, San Francisco: three girls, two boys, and a baby. He painted them in the Marine Hotel, North Berwick, charging £55 each. Apprehensive about painting the baby, he was pleased when it turned out the best. With the two commissions he was able to bank £430—a good year's earnings for three months' work. The year was beginning to improve, and continued well as, on his way

32. Portrait of Horatio Forbes Brown, oil, 1899. R314.
(present whereabouts unknown).

33. *Rounding the Manacle Buoy*, oil, 1888. R108. (Tuke Collection, RCPS).

34.   *The Message*, oil, 1890. R152. (Falmouth Art Gallery/Falmouth Town Council).

through London, he painted *Mrs Lawrence*, the daughter of Vice-Chancellor Judge Frank Bacon, former Chief Judge in Bankruptcy (who had been one of his first sitters obtained by Dowdeswell eight years earlier: then his price had been sixty guineas; now it was seventy).

He was also commissioned by his family to do pastel portraits of his paternal great-grandfather (Henry Tuke 1755-1814) and his grandfather (Samuel Tuke 1784-1857) for presentation to the York Retreat. Recalling the Quaker beliefs about paintings, this commission was perhaps especially pleasant, implying a particular tribute to their artist descendant.

Returning to Falmouth, he sold *The Steering Lesson*, his poignant and well-observed picture of Neddy Hall and his small son Freddy, done originally for an Australian commission but then unsold. He decided that he deserved and could well afford a holiday, and his thoughts (after an unseasonably wet and destructive spring in Falmouth) turned to the warm south, and Italy.

The Dalrymples were going to Lady Dalrymple's villa at Monte Carlo, and in February Tuke travelled down with Walter Dalrymple, pausing as usual in Paris to take in the exhibitions. At Genoa he was able to row round the harbour and walk the quay sketching the ships. Then he travelled to Venice to stay with a new friend, Horatio Forbes Brown.

The year before, Brown had bought a Tuke at Dowdeswell's June show of the results of his spring trawl to Newlyn and Falmouth. It was *Spanish Boy in the Rigging*, and Brown paid £9 for it. He was on his customary summer visit from Venice, where he shared a palazzo with his mother, and was employed by the British government to catalogue the Venetian State Papers from the viewpoint of British interests. Mrs Brown was a Forbes; she had married a rich Scottish landowner much older than herself who had died leaving her with two small sons and a fortune. The Browns moved to Florence as an economy, but finding it full of Forbeses, went to Venice. There Horatio, a

> fair-haired, breezy, out-of-doors person with a crisp Highland-Scottish speech . . . made the acquaintance of a gondolier, Antonio Salin, whom he transported with his family to the back parts of his house which he called Casa Torresella. He saw Venice through the eyes of his gondolier and his gondolier's friends, with whom he spent much of his time, playing *tre sette* (a game of cards) and *bocce* (bowls) and drinking the wine of Padua at an *osteria* behind the house.[51]

Brown translated Antonio's knowledge of the 'real' Venice into a series of readable and informative books[52] that were eagerly bought by visitors; and he became a good and cheerful friend to Tuke, as did his mother, whose portrait Tuke painted on a later visit.

It was a leisurely holiday. Tuke spent the morning sight-seeing, then after lunch they went out in the *sandolo* to the Lagoon, 'all of us rowing', returning for dinner. From Venice, he went across to Florence where the Gotches were living, and then to Siena and Rome: all the time he was sketching. The remainder of his five-month holiday was spent in Corfu with Arthur Tanner and a friend.

> Once more living the old savage life [he wrote to his sister], a relief after so much sightseeing and respectable clothes.[53]

But in Corfu he began to paint again (*A Corfu Garden*, now known as *The Lemon Tree*, and *Greek Lemon Gatherer*). Evidently his energy and strength were returning.

In his absence, he was represented in the Royal Academy by two portraits, *Mrs Lawrence* and *Lady Hamilton-Dalrymple*. He sailed back to England with Arthur Tanner in July. Once back home, he welcomed visitors, among them John Addington Symonds, who was visiting Britain that summer from his home in Switzerland—ostensibly to deliver a lecture by invitation at Oxford on the Renaissance.[54] Symonds brought with him his favourite Venetian gondolier, the handsome Antonio Fusato, whom he had met while staying with Horatio Brown. He travelled around the country to visit friends—among them Lord Ronald Gower. One of his visits was to Falmouth, to meet Tuke. They had several points of contact, not least that their fathers, both doctors, had known each other (and Dr Tuke had visited Symonds in Switzerland). They shared a friend in Horatio Brown, and Tuke can have been in no doubt about the impulse that had led Symonds to write to him two years earlier:

> I want to tell you how much I admire . . . your *Perseus* . . . The feeling for the nude in it seems to me as delicate as it is vigorous. I wish you would . . . send me some photographs of your various pictures and studies.[55]

In September he went to Falmouth lodging in a hotel, but taking a moonlit walk with Tuke, and then spending two days at the Swanpool cottage. Whether it was as a result of Symonds' sage

35. Outside Tuke's house. From left to right: Lindsay Symington, Everard Meynell, Tuke and Johnny Jackett. c.1896. (Private Collection).

counsel or the invigorating effect of his trip to Italy, Corfu and Albania, Tuke's new-found artistic freedom exploded on to the canvas in a painting which had all the 'truth and beauty of flesh in sunlight by the sea'.[56] Painted in Falmouth Bay in the fine summer of 1893, *August Blue* was the sensation of the 1894 Academy, and confounded Symonds' expectations that naturalism wouldn't pay, by becoming the second of Tuke's paintings to be purchased for the nation by the Chantrey Bequest, this time for £525. 'Swelled head', its owner recorded laconically in his diary, with some justification for, as his sister confirmed, 'it was then an almost unprecedented compliment for any artist to have two pictures bought by the Chantrey'.[57] Others whose work had found similar favour included Lord Leighton, then President of the Royal Academy, and Frank Dicksee (who was President much later), but Tuke's achievement was particularly remarkable as he had not yet been nominated for membership of the Royal Academy.

Despite an absence (apart from occasional visits) of almost a decade from Newlyn, Tuke was still regarded as a member of that group of artists, having indeed been referred to as one by his cousin-by-marriage, the poet Alice Meynell, in her pioneering article on the Newlyn School in 1889:

And seeing that some Newlyners abide at St

Ives . . . and that one dwells in a boat off Falmouth, their nickname is assuredly given them in acknowledgement of something they have in common.[58]

Nevertheless it is noticeable that Tuke's closest friends amongst the artistic communities in Cornwall were those who also reserved a certain detachment in their relationships with Newlyn. William Ayerst Ingram (one of the St Ives 'Newlyners' referred to above) moved to Falmouth in the early 1890s, and remained one of Tuke's closest friends until his death in 1913; and Tuke's old classmate at the Slade, Tom Gotch, was already spending much time abroad pursuing his individual brand of decorative 'imaginative symbolism'. As Stanhope Forbes had described (admittedly not to their faces) Tom's wife, Carrie, disapprovingly as 'very aesthetic and untidy', and considered Gotch himself to be 'a weak sort of creature', comparing him rather unkindly to an unmade bed,[59] it is perhaps hardly surprising that the Gotches, while maintaining a residence in Newlyn, preferred not to become too involved with the other artists in the town. Tuke himself stressed the Falmouth contingent's artistic independence from Newlyn:

We consider ourselves quite a distinct branch of the brotherhood, and we are a very congenial set, too.[60]

36.   *Two Children on Deck*, oil, *c*.1890. (Tuke Collection, RCPS).

37.   *The Steering Lesson*, oil, 1892. R183. (Private Collection).

With *August Blue*, Tuke signalled his own loosening of the bonds which had linked him to the Newlyn group, although throughout his life he adhered to the overriding principle of *plein air* painting which united them all. Gone was the feeling that the picture must tell a story; the title, taken from Swinburne's poem 'Sundew', was not an illustration of the poem but of the images evoked by the two words. (The sundew is 'a little marsh-plant, yellow green, And pricked at lip with tender red . . .'—Tuke's colours, of course.) Though Tuke never followed Symonds' suggestion that his pictures should be numbered instead of being given titles, *August Blue* was the first in a series of paintings which, following Whistler, took their names from their predominating colours instead of their subjects: others were *Ruby, Gold and Malachite; Green and Gold* and *Aquamarine*.

Also new was the absence of the softly atmospheric pearly light, so beloved of the Newlyn artists that it was said some would even refuse an invitation to a dance for fear of missing the one grey day in the week.[61] Here overcast weather gives way to skies of Mediterranean blue with the sun blazing down, setting the pattern for most of Tuke's bathing pictures in the years to come.

Tuke's Register lists six names for those who posed for the four figures in *August Blue*, the reverse of his earlier usage (the same boy often appearing more than once in the same painting), and is an indication that his problems in finding models—male ones, at least—were finally over. Certainly his popularity among the men and boys on the waterfront was unquestioned as an article in the *Windsor Magazine* in 1895 affirmed:

You have only to mention his name to the boatmen on the quay, and, in their downright Cornish fashion, they seem as if they cannot sufficiently praise him.[62]

Tuke was scrupulous in asking permission from a boy's parents before inviting him to act as a model, and as by spending their summers fishing, swimming naked in the sea,[63] or messing about in boats, his young models were simply doing what they would have done anyway in their leisure hours—the only difference being that they were paid, albeit modestly, for it—no objections appear to have been raised. Tuke evidently became more considerate of his models' welfare as the years passed;[64] in *August Blue*, he had two sets of models, and 'when one set got perished with the cold they were relieved, and the others went on duty'.[65]

The resulting composite figures give his treatment of the nude an impersonality and detachment which is one of the most characteristic hallmarks of Tuke's mature style.

Obtaining female models was a very different matter. While local girls—such as the lovely Emmeline Clift (later Mrs Arthur Brown), the daughter of an old friend made during the Tuke family's earlier stay in Falmouth—could 'lend their heads' for paintings when required,[66] to paint a female nude involved employing a professional model from London and finding her suitable lodgings in Falmouth. The long walk out to Swanpool, as well as the 'dullness' of life in Falmouth compared to London apparently deterred several potential models—both male and female—and with enough local boys now willing to be painted in return for a small fee, it is hardly surprising that Tuke seldom felt that the additional effort and expense of using professional models of either sex was worthwhile.

The subterfuge entailed in painting female nudes was recounted by George Jacomb-Hood, who stayed with Tuke in 1895.

There was one pleasant summer with my friend near Falmouth, when he was engaged on a picture of the Mermaid and the Fisherboy [*The Mermaid's Cave*, R 239]. The scene was a cave [at Meudon, beyond Maenporth Beach] about a mile along the coast, only to be entered at low-tide; the mermaid was a young girl-model from London, who was put up with a good couple in Falmouth, and who spent the day with us, rowing round to the cave and 'posing' as the mermaid therein, when the tide allowed. To silence the curiosity of Tuke's Falmouth friends, she was supposed to be my niece. Lily Purl (that was her name) had the time of her life. We got her a bathing-dress and taught her to swim and handle a boat. Strangely enough, her father was a Mormon missionary in London, travelling about the country, generally in Wales, where he made converts. She and her family returned to Salt Lake City soon afterwards, where we learnt that she developed a fine soprano voice and was training as a singer.[67]

The rejection of *The Mermaid's Cave* for the 1896 Academy was a bitter disappointment for Tuke, especially after his successes in previous years, and was hardly compensated for by the acceptance of the painting in Munich and then at the Paris Salon in the following year. An insight into the reasons for its rejection by the Academy has been given by Sallie Jackett, the widow of Johnny

38. Tuke and Johnny
Jackett, c.1896.
(Private Collection).

seasonal boatman and as a model, appearing in at least eight major paintings over a twelve-year period, and numerous smaller studies. An outstanding athlete, being cycling champion of Cornwall several times in the 1890s, Johnny Jackett was to achieve lasting fame as a rugby footballer, captaining the Cornish XV many times, and playing (at full-back) for England on thirteen occasions between 1905 and 1909.

Tuke tried never to miss a match in which Johnny was playing, and in return Johnny's devotion to Tuke was complete; according to Maria, 'I think John would have allowed himself to be flayed alive if it could have done Harry any good',[70] an opinion supported by Jackett's wife: 'John put him above everyone. There was something about Mr Tuke which was entirely different to anyone else'.[71]

In 1900 Tuke's Venetian friend Horatio Brown published (in London) a slim book of verses entitled *Drift*. Two of the poems derived from Brown's visits to Swanpool (see Appendix II). One—reminiscent of Marlowe's passionate shepherd— was entitled 'Johnnie Jacket', its last verse running:

> Hie! Johnnie Jacket!
> Ho! Johnnie Jacket!
> Young Johnnie Jacket,
> Come and live wi' me;
> For life may be a folly,
> But we two will make it jolly,
> If we sail and swim together, and can live like you and me.

As an expression of Johnny Jackett's cheerful companionship it was no doubt innocent enough, though Jackett's opinion of it can only be guessed. Tuke recognised that Johnny would probably marry; and when he did, Tuke made his wife Sallie completely welcome. She recalled that

> Mr Tuke never passed me once in all the years I knew him. If I was on one side of the road and he on the other he always came across and said 'Where are you off to, Sallie? . . .' [They were] lovely, lovely times . . . I thought it was the greatest compliment that could ever be paid to anyone, when he said he was pleased I'd married John, and John had improved wonderfully, less selfish.[72]

Sallie remembered one occasion when some friend of Tuke's had upset Johnny by touching him when he was posing nude. The man (unidentified other than as 'a well-known Falmouth author') touched his arm, 'and [John]

Jackett who was the model for the nude fisherboy lying on his stomach holding his chin up in his hands. When the painting was hung in the Academy, standing away from it, it looked as if the boy's face was against her flesh, so they refused to keep it there. Can you think of anything more narrow-minded? Considering that it took every honour it was possible to take in France . . .[68]

Johnny Jackett had first modelled for Tuke, at the age of sixteen, in *The Swimmers' Pool* the previous year. Tuke had no doubt met him earlier since his father was a local boat-builder who was then working on Tuke's latest sailing vessel (in the one-rater class), the *Red Heart*. Described by Maria as 'a very intelligent boy, who could do anything, either in the studio or the boats',[69] he soon became indispensable to Tuke both as

39. *The Lemon Tree* (also known as *A Corfu Garden*), oil, 1892. R187. (Bradford City Art Galleries and Museums.)

40. Head of Johnny Jackett, oil, 1899. R273. (Roy Miles Gallery, London).

thought that was an accident. The second time it happened, he just pulled the towel or dressing gown around him and said "I'm going up, Mr Tuke". . . . "Mr Tuke told me I was ridiculous".[73] That Johnny was the last person to respond to any male proposition has been confirmed by his wife:

> Of course John had 1001 girl friends, and do you know what he said to me? . . . I remember repeating it to Mr Tuke . . . He said 'I never had an affair with a woman in my life unless I was positive I was in love with her . . . I always ask[ed], I had plenty of noes and plenty of yesses.' . . . Mr Tuke laughed till he cried . . . he said 'That was the John, that was the real Johnny I knew'.[74]

On one occasion, Tuke even had to intervene to extricate Johnny from a scrape involving a former girlfriend, a coastguard's daughter from Portscatho whom he had made pregnant, and who alleged that Johnny had failed to keep his promise to marry her. The baby had been born in September 1899 but had died before the case came to court in the following February. Johnny made no attempt to deny his liability but in his defence claimed that the 'precarious living' he earned as model and servant to Mr Tuke for seven months in the year (eight shillings per week with board and lodging — compared with the eight shillings a day that professional models in London could expect to earn — and nothing at all during the five months each year that Tuke spent away from Falmouth) made it impossible for him to make any contribution to the girl. Nevertheless, damages assessed at £150 were awarded against Johnny, and it was not until a year had passed, during which he failed — or perhaps was genuinely unable — to make any payments, that Tuke came to his rescue by testifying in court to Johnny's financial situation and agreeing to advance him the required sum. Johnny's own wages were cut to three shillings a week to compensate, but the loan may never have been repaid in full, as within two months of the case being resolved — possibly feeling that a judicious period of absence was called for — Johnny signed up with the Kimberley Mounted Police and left Falmouth to take part in the Boer War.[75]

Johnny Jackett was totally loyal and devoted to Tuke, and there is no doubt that in Tuke's eyes Johnny was the dearest companion he ever had. They swam together, sailed together, cycled together; Johnny's calm, solid reliability came to mean much to Tuke. Johnny told his wife that 'Mr Tuke was everything that was wonderful'. But it is clear that the relationship between them, of deep

41. Sallie and Johnny Jackett with Tuke on the beach at Falmouth, c.1920. (Private Collection).

love on both sides, was entirely asexual. This was difficult for Tuke's homosexual friends to accept.

On the other hand, Horatio Brown's sonnet about Pennance with its reference to '. . . love serene, erect, robust and grand . . .' is much more equivocal. It is true that Brown's book of verses had a very limited circulation. It is also evident that Tuke was well aware of the romantic passions that Johnny Jackett aroused in some of his friends. John Gambril Nicholson, whom Tuke often met at Kains Jackson's, wrote his poem 'Ballade of the Stadium' in his book *A Garland of Ladslove* for Tuke about Jackett at Kensal Rise cycle track, during his days as a racing cyclist.[76]

Tuke's diaries give little indication about his own emotions, the entries consisting mainly of clipped, factual records of where he went and whom he saw. But just occasionally there is an entry that suggests his reactions:

> February 5, 1900 . . . To 'Our Navy' Biograph [an early film show] at the Poly. Some most entrancing things.[77]

The Swimmers' Pool had been produced under difficult circumstances — 'interrupted every few minutes by clouds or rain and the models shivering and fidgety' — and while finishing off the painting in the early spring of 1895, in preparation for that year's Academy, Tuke was dealt a serious blow by the news of the sudden illness of his father, and after only a few days he died at the age of sixty-seven. The *Dictionary of Psychological Medicine*, with which Daniel Hack Tuke, as the book's main contributor, had consolidated his already high reputation as one of the country's leading physicians specialising in mental illness, had been published less than three years earlier. His influence on English psychiatry was afterwards described as 'inestimable'.[78] Tuke hurried home in time to see his father before he died, and stayed on as long as he could to give some comfort to his mother and sister. He had been very close to his father, despite their occasional differences of opinion, and in after years would relate, with obvious pride, chance meetings he had had with medical men who had read Dr Tuke's books and followed his distinguished career.[79]

His sister Maria being increasingly occupied with her growing family,[80] Tuke's sense of responsibility towards his mother became noticeably greater. For the twenty-two years that she survived her husband, Tuke spent most of each winter with her at Hanwell. They saw in each New Year together while staying with their Saffron Walden cousins. His custom was to spend Boxing Day making hand-painted 'New Year cards', about 3in by 5in, for his friends. Usually of ships, they would be made in some quantity by a production-line technique. He would set them out along a table, load his brush with watercolour, and then dab one colour on each—a red sail, a green hull, a blue sea. His friends greatly valued these delightful miniatures. Tuke also ensured that his mother enjoyed numerous Cornish

holidays, staying usually in the homes of different branches of the Fox family in the beautiful countryside around Falmouth.

The Swimmers' Pool sold before the Academy even opened, for another record sum: £600. Only one other painting—*Midsummer Morning* in 1908—was to be sold in Tuke's lifetime for a higher figure. Writing seven years after it had been exhibited, Kains Jackson still thought that *The Swimmers' Pool* was the finest work Tuke had so far produced. 'It has that sense of inevitability about it which only quite first-rate work enjoys.'[81] Tuke was now exhibiting on average one bathing picture each year at the Royal Academy, the only exception being 1896, the year *The Mermaid's Cave* was rejected. In 1897 the bathing picture was *Beside Green Waters*. Innovatively, it was painted from a pontoon of logs, to give the picture a foreground of deep water. He was happy with the result:

> Am getting keen about my new picture . . . The subject is a most beautiful arrangement of flesh and grey rock with a little deep green water in the front, quite unlike any others.[82]

Some sterner critics were beginning to detect an 'inevitability' in his work which they assessed in less flattering terms. *The Diver*, though separated by four years from *The Swimmers' Pool*, shares with it similarities in the arrangement of five boys (Johnny Jackett again the principal model) in and around a dinghy in the shallow rock-strewn water of Newporth Beach, and in the pose in both paintings of the reclining figure in the boat nonchalantly dangling one leg over the side. It was hung on the line at the Royal Academy in 1899, and attracted the following comments from a local reviewer:

> It is one of those daring studies which would daunt the majority of painters, yet Mr Tuke seems to find nothing so congenial to his mind as to tackle a subject everybody else would shrink from . . . Masterly as is Mr Tuke's work, one cannot help feeling regret that he does not give his attention to a more acceptable subject. He is, in the opinion of those competent to judge, the strongest artist outside the Academy circle, and there can be no doubt that had he confined himself to the canons of modern art . . . he would have been admitted as an Associate of the Royal Academy years ago . . .[83]

Given this sort of criticism, Tuke's election to Associate Membership of the Royal Academy less

42. Tuke with his sister, Maria's, children at Mawnan Smith, Falmouth, *c.*1902. From left to right: Hester, Willy, Geoffrey and Philip. (Private Collection).

43. *Cupid and Sea Nymphs*, oil, 1898-99. R306. (Collection a descendant of George Beldam).

44. Four New Year cards painted by Tuke, watercolour. (Private Collection).

45.   *August Blue*, oil, 1893. R210. (Tate Gallery, London).

than a year later must have been particularly gratifying to him, setting the seal of official approval on his work. The announcement appears to have been unexpected; Tuke was staying in Tunbridge Wells, where he was putting the finishing touches to a portrait of *Miss Ethel Court*, and the first he knew of his success was by reading of it in the newspaper before breakfast on 31 January 1900, the morning after his election had taken place. The *Chronicle of Art*, in its announcement, added the comment that

> Mr Tuke's admirable realism, his conscientious ability, and almost unerring taste, have become familiar to the public through his pictures of West England sea-board and land-scape, and his finely-drawn figures.[84]

Back in London, the congratulations started to flood in, from fellow artists such as John Singer Sargent and George Clausen—'It is good for the RA as well as you'—and from friends. Horatio Brown wrote:

You have the satisfaction of knowing that it was fully deserved, and you never raised a finger to help yourself win it, except by your painting.[85]

It was the reception given to the news by his adopted home town, however, which brought him most pleasure. He returned to Falmouth as soon as he had carried out the expected rounds of calls to Academicians ('the first duty of the elect'), which included visits to some of the giants of Victorian painting, such as W.P.(*Derby Day*) Frith and Sir Lawrence Alma-Tadema.[86] On 14 February Tuke wrote in his diary:

> A lovely day ending up with my banquet which Ingram & Downing, Knutson & Masson Fox got up. The Polytechnic Hall well decorated with flags & bunting & daffodils all up the tables. About 43 present & all went swimmingly. Lionel Birch and his wife gave a little entertainment, & Wicks's string band from Truro discoursed the whiles we were feeding. Robert Fox in the chair.

46. *The Diver*, oil, 1898. R307. This painting is said to have disappeared in the 1930s from the pictures sent for sale by the family. (present whereabouts unknown).

A fuller account of the occasion was sent to Tuke's mother by the wife of his friend John Downing:

The tables were beautifully decorated by Mr Ingram and my husband, no ladies took any part in the decorating at all. Mr Ingram took a lot of trouble to design a valentine for Mr Tuke which was in front of his table at supper . . . Mr Robert Fox in his speech made some reference to his wish that Mr Tuke could find someone to share his honours, which, to say the least, was embarrassing, but the object of it all quietly helped himself to a *meringue au Jean Paul Laurens.* Can you not almost see him? At the end after cheers for the Queen, everyone gave three hearty cheers for Mr Tuke. I believe everyone here is delighted with this election and an occasion like this enables one to see how much Mr Tuke is liked in our little town.[87]

The menu, into which references to the various stages of Tuke's career and to his many interests are ingeniously woven, was as follows:

47. Portrait of Esther Wyatt, oil, 1900. R333. (present whereabouts unknown).

BANQUET

Complimentaire à Mons. H S TUKE, A.R.A.

POLYTECHNIC HALL, FEB. 14TH, 1900

Potage à la Swanpool
Cotelettes et Petits Pois à la Pennance
Boeuf à l'Associate
Agneau Roti à l'Académie Royale
Poulet au Firefly   Poulet au Menemopote
Langue au Coeur Rouge
Galantine aux garçons baignants
Pâté d'Euchre   Plante Marine
Bouilleurs aux pots   Medusée au Madère
Boudin Tout le Monde aux Pompes
Meringues au Jean Paul Laurens
Oeuf modele   Brosses de Peintre
Dessert   Café[88]

The Royal Cornwall Polytechnic Society, in whose premises the banquet was held, had been established in 1833 'for the object of encouraging Mechanical and Scientific Inventions, and also the Fine and Industrial Arts'.[89] It had been the brainchild of Anna Maria Fox and her sister Caroline, teenage daughters of the eminent scientist and inventor, Robert Were Fox, FSA.

Tuke's association with the Royal Cornwall Polytechnic Society began in 1890 when he and Ingram helped to organise an exhibition of 'the finest collection of modern pictures shown in the Hall for many years'.[90] Like many of the great nineteenth century institutions, the 'Poly' fell into gradual decline during the early part of the twentieth century, but the influence it had exerted, and continued to exert, over artistic and scientific awareness in the region meant that Tuke's election as a Vice-President of the Society in 1899 was still a considerable honour.

Earlier, in 1897, he had been invited to paint the portrait of the Society's co-founder, the rather formidable-looking Miss Anna Maria Fox, who Maria remembered from her childhood attending Quaker meetings with a little bright-eyed marmoset nestled on her arm.[91] Aged eighty-one when Tuke began the portrait in July, she died only four months after its completion. The sittings were attended by younger members of the family and by Miss Fox's servants, who all helped by reading aloud or talking to the old lady to prevent sleepiness overcoming her. Tuke noted in his Register that the book read aloud during these sittings was Mahon's *Nelson*, also *Lord Roberts and the Delectable Duchess*. On other occasions, different sitters were treated to Jane Austen's *Emma* and *Northanger Abbey*, and Miss Thackeray's *Village on the Cliff*.[92]

Sitting to Tuke for one's portrait appears to have been a pleasantly relaxed experience, and those of his sitters with whom he was not already acquainted often became lasting friends. Tuke was a good conversationalist, with wide-ranging interests and an open mind, and he was also a

younger artist sometimes imitating the colours he used, as well as his fluid and impressionistic style. The consummately-handled portrait of *Lady Agnew* (National Gallery of Scotland) exhibited at the Royal Academy in 1893, was clearly the inspiration for Tuke's own much-praised portrait of *Mrs George Talbot*, shown two years later—even to the studied casual gracefulness of the pose of both women leaning back against one

sympathetic listener. After painting Mrs Genn, the Town Clerk's wife, during his early years in Falmouth, he wrote: 'What a nice woman she is, as usual with sitters alone she has been very confidential and told me a good many of her troubles'.[93] Towards the end of his career, Tuke painted the eminent judge, Sir Arthur Channell, in his studio at Swanpool, and came to the end of their sittings with regret: 'Have enjoyed our conversations very much & found the Judge a delightful companion'.[94]

Tuke's restful presence was in marked contrast to that of his famous contemporary John Singer Sargent, who found painting female portraits especially daunting: 'Women don't ask you to make them beautiful, but you can feel them wanting you to do so all the time'.[95] In portraiture, Sargent was the painter Tuke most admired, the

arm of an elegant drawing-room chair—like Sargent's painting, 'a beautiful scheme of pale heliotrope and white'.[96]

Tuke frequently recorded his admiration for Sargent, usually with reference to his annual Academy exhibits: in 1901 after the Varnishing Day, 'Sargent's Miss[es] Wertheimer & Hemy's sea apparently about the best things', in 1905, a touch wistfully, 'Sargent as usual predominating', and again in 1906, 'Sargent as usual dominated the show'. He never tried to match the scope of Sargent's works; by contrast his portraits remained on a relatively small scale, reassuringly human, with his female portraits often the most intimate of all.

Most of Tuke's portraiture was undertaken during the winter in London and elsewhere away from Cornwall, but some of those he carried out

48. *The Missionary Boat*, oil, 1894. R209. The boat was the French barque *Verveine* with the British Sailors' Society Chaplain, James Badger, going alongside. (Tuke Collection, RCPS).

49. Portrait of Mrs Humphris, oil, 1892. R176. (Tate Gallery, London).

of his friends in Falmouth are worthy of attention, notably the small half-length of *Mrs Humphris*, wife of an artist friend. Painted as early as 1892, it was not shown at the Royal Academy until 1914, the year of his election to full membership, and is one of his most appealing character studies. A particularly close friend of Tuke during the 1890s, Mrs Humphris was according to Maria the confidante of all the young artists in Falmouth and their friends at the time, as well as being a charming and hospitable hostess. Doubtless she was also behind many attempts to matchmake for Tuke, a personable bachelor, but if this was the case, she was doomed to failure; after observing a recently-married couple of his acquaintance, Tuke said firmly:

> They seem exceedingly attached and blissful, all the same I don't envy them, and when I get out of the gate I thank my stars I still walk alone. My two earliest declarations that I would be an artist and a bachelor hold true so far.[97]

Another local venture with which Tuke was concerned, together with Ingram and Downing, was the setting up in 1894 of the Falmouth Art Gallery. Exhibitions were held annually, at any time between June and November, in the Gallery's premises at Grovehill. To begin with, the exhibitors were limited to a short list of artists selected by the Directors (in 1899 confined to Hemy, Ingram, Tuke and his cousin Henry Rheam), but by the early years of the century the exhibitions seem to have become more open. Lindsay Symington, a frequent visitor over a period of thirty years, exhibited some of his early pastels there and soon after had work accepted at the Royal Academy.

Tuke's own involvement with the Gallery, apart from helping annually to arrange the exhibits, was rather less than Ingram's, and even in 1894 he seemed to be regretting having taken on the responsibility.

> I should be very pleased to get rid of my share in it. Ingram is still very keen, and thinks me horribly apathetic, as I am, and as I remind him I told him I should be.[98]

Ingram was clearly the most energetic member of Falmouth's small artistic community, 'Tregurrian'—the comfortable home of himself and his hospitable American wife—becoming their accepted meeting place. Gotch was a regular visitor there while carrying out various portrait commissions (the two artists affectionately

addressing each other as 'Sir Thomas' and 'Sir Ayerst'), and in October 1899 the American painter Alexander Harrison, whose practice of painting nudes in the open air in the orchards of France had been so formative an influence on Tuke's own work, stayed with Ingram for a couple of days after visiting some former associates at St Ives.

As a means of disposing of his smaller sketches, the Gallery proved to be quite lucrative for Tuke, although he had no particular need of another outlet for his work in Falmouth, as by the mid-nineties he had his own studio in a converted building a few yards behind his house, which attracted a steady trickle of visitors. In 1898 he had a new studio built adjacent to the house (the old one being converted to a billiard room: yet another game in which Tuke delighted—in London he used often to go and watch the classic billiards and snooker games in Leicester Square). In October 1899 he held a party to inaugurate the new studio. Assembling a corps of willing ladies to tidy the studio and prepare and serve the food, Tuke himself spent the day hanging Japanese lanterns.[99]

When not painting, Tuke's main form of recreation was still sailing. He was a founder member of the Falmouth Sailing Club, set up in 1894 to encourage cruising and small boat racing, and became its Vice-Commodore in 1898. The Club virtually ceased to exist after 1912 when Tuke left it to join the more élite Royal Cornwall Yacht Club. He had every opportunity to gain racing experience, for his diary shows that in the first few years of the new century as much of his time in Falmouth was spent sailing as it was in painting. A typical summer's day would find him painting on the beach in the morning, often starting as early as six o'clock, until lunchtime, and then spending the rest of the day sailing, perhaps taking part in one of the many town or village regattas which were a feature of high summer in Cornwall, or in Sailing Club or Royal Cornwall Yacht Club races, before returning in the evening to dine out with friends. Most of his many visitors over the course of each summer joined in this pleasant routine with enjoyment, though Tuke occasionally resented their intrusion into time he felt would have been better spent painting.

1   Maria Tuke Sainsbury, p.75
2   Henry Scott Tuke Registers (R 51)
3   Flora Klickmann, 'The Life Story of a Famous Painter'—An Interview with Mr Henry Scott Tuke, *Windsor Magazine*, 1895, p. 606
4   Maria Tuke Sainsbury, p.76
5   So called after the chimney stacks used to expel arsenic fumes from the long-disused silver smelting works on the cliffs at Pennance
6   Maria Tuke Sainsbury, p.76
7   *ibid*
8   Maria Tuke Sainsbury, p.77
9   Flora Klickmann, *op. cit.*, p.606
10 Graham Reynolds, *Victorian Painting*, Studio Vista, 1966, p.194
11 Frank Bramley painted one of the best-loved of all Victorian genre paintings, *A Hopeless Dawn* (Tate Gallery), which is set in a Newlyn cottage
12 Graham Reynolds, *op. cit.*, p.194. Maria Tuke Sainsbury (p.77) confuses *The Bathers* with *Two Falmouth Fisher Boys*, whereas they are in fact two different paintings
13 Alfred Thornton, *Fifty Years of the New English Art Club*, printed for the Club by the Curwen Press, 1935
14 Stanhope Forbes' letter to his mother, 14 Aug 1885 (quoted in Caroline Fox and Francis Greenacre, *Artists of the Newlyn School 1880-1900*, exhibition catalogue published by Newlyn Orion Galleries, 1979, p.132)
15 Dr. James Whetter, *The History of Falmouth*, Dyllansow Truran, 1981, pp.66-70
16 Edwin T. Olver, *Falmouth and its Surroundings* (official Guide) 1910-11, pp.4-5
17 Lt-Col. C. J. H. Mead, *History of the Royal Cornwall Yacht Club 1871-1949*, printed privately, 1949
18 Maria Tuke Sainsbury, p.77
19 *ibid*, p.81
20 *ibid*
21 *ibid*, p.82
22 Caroline Fox and Francis Greenacre, *Painting in Newlyn*, Barbican Art Gallery, 1985, p.101
23 Reminiscences: interview with Sallie Jackett recorded by Brian D. Price on 30 May 1965, p.28
24 *Charles Napier Hemy, RA 1841-1917*, exhibition catalogue published by Tyne and Wear County Council Museums, 1984, p.47
25 Reminiscences: interview with Henry Allen recorded by Brian D. Price on 27 March 1965, p.2
26 Maria Tuke Sainsbury, pp.128-9
27 *Charles Napier Hemy, op. cit.*, pp.17-27
28 Stanhope Forbes to his mother, 18 Oct 1888 (quoted by Fox and Greenacre, Newlyn Orion catalogue *op. cit.*, p.135)
29 Artists' Letters: Mrs Judith Shilling to Henry Scott Tuke, 9 Oct 1887, and Walter Shilling to Henry Scott Tuke, 26 Oct 1887, Nos.164 and 165, pp.141-2. 'Tea-treats'—a long-established Cornish custom—were originally outings arranged for young members of the Church and Sunday schools
30 Maria Tuke Sainsbury, p.85
31 The painting was sub-titled *The Dog Watch*, the nickname for the short afternoon or early evening watch (4-6, or 6-8 pm) on board ship
32 Maria Tuke Sainsbury, p.86
33 Charles Kains Jackson, 'Henry Scott Tuke, ARA', *The Magazine of Art, op. cit.*, p.338
34 Yeames is now best-remembered for introducing a cliché to the English language, through his painting *And when did you last see your father?* (Walker Art Gallery, Liverpool)
35 Flora Klickmann, *op. cit.*, p.608
36 It has been suggested (Timothy d'Arch Smith, *Love in Earnest*, Routledge & Kegan Paul, p.60) that Cecil Castle modelled (with Willy Rowling and Albert Pidwell) for Tuke's 1888 painting *Bathers* (R 114), which was illustrated in The *Artist* in 1889, although he is not named in the Registers
37 Maria Tuke Sainsbury, p.88
38 Maria Tuke Sainsbury, p.98
39 A full account of the devastation wreaked around the coasts of Cornwall and Devon, and inland, may be found in Clive Carter, *The Blizzard of '91*, David & Charles, 1971
40 Maria Tuke Sainsbury, p.92
41 *ibid*, p.94
42 Artists' Letters: Jack Rolling to Henry Scott Tuke, ? 15 Jan 1890
43 Dramatic photographs of *SS Mohegan* going down may be seen in the Falmouth Art Gallery
44 From a letter written in October 1898, Maria Tuke Sainsbury, p.93
45 *ibid*, 6 Nov 1898; Maria Tuke Sainsbury, p.93-4
46 Obituary of Mr J. G. Rowling, ? *Falmouth Packet*, c.1909
47 The legend of the beautiful youth who perished in his attempt to swim across the Hellespont for love of the goddess Hero was one which held an obvious attraction for Tuke
48 E. Bonning Steyne, 'Afternoons in Studios: Henry Scott Tuke at Falmouth', *Studio* magazine, 1895, p.94
49 Notably Charles Kains Jackson: see his article in the *Magazine of Art, op. cit.*, p.340
50 From a letter from J. A. Symonds to Henry Scott Tuke, 10 Jan 1893, quoted in Maria Tuke Sainsbury, p.107
51 *Directory of National Biography*: Horatio Brown
52 Horatio Brown, *Life on the Lagoons*, 1884; *Venetian Studies*, 1887; *In and Round Venice*, 1905, etc.
53 Maria Tuke Sainsbury, p.100
54 Phyllis Grosskurth, *John Addington Symonds*, Longman 1964, pp.311-12
55 Maria Tuke Sainsbury, p.106
56 E. Bonning Steyne, *Studio, op. cit.*, p.94
57 Maria Tuke Sainsbury, p.112

58 Alice Meynell, 'Newlyn', *Art Journal*, 1889, p.99 (quoted in Fox and Greenacre, Newlyn Orion catalogue *op. cit.*, p.131)

59 Stanhope Forbes to his mother, 15 Oct 1886 (quoted in Fox and Greenacre, *op. cit.*, p.175)

60 Flora Klickmann, *op. cit.*, p.608-9

61 Michael Jacobs, *The Good and Simple Life: Artist Colonies in Europe and America*, Phaidon, 1985, p.148

62 Flora Klickmann, *op. cit.*, p.602

63 The custom of wearing special clothing for bathing is of comparatively short duration, especially among working-class youths, to whom the possession of such a garment would have been regarded as an unnecessary luxury and hence as an object of derision. In Falmouth, mixed bathing came into fashion towards the turn of the century, taking place officially only on designated beaches where a certain amount of segregation of the sexes still applied. The rustic genre scenes by leading Victorian and Edwardian photographers, such as F. Sutcliffe and P. H. Emerson, indicate that the practice of nude bathing by boys and young men was widespread, and even as recently as the 1930s, sections of both the Cam and the Isis were traditionally regarded as being kept for this purpose by local youths, under-graduates and young (and not so young) dons.

64 Flora Klickmann, *op. cit.*, p.606

65 *ibid*

66 Emmeline Clift 'lent her . . . head' (Maria's words) for *The First Boat In* (R75); Maria Tuke Sainsbury, p.78

67 G. P. Jacomb-Hood, *With Brush and Pencil*, Murray, 1925, (quoted in Henry Scott Tuke Registers under R239)

68 Reminiscences: interview with Sallie Jackett recorded by Brian D. Price on 23 May 1965, p.26

69 Maria Tuke Sainsbury, p.114

70 Maria Tuke Sainsbury, p.123

71 Reminiscences: interview with Sallie Jackett recorded by Brian D. Price on 23 May 1965, p.25

72 *ibid*, p.37

73 *ibid*

74 *ibid*, p.30

75 Details of the Breach of Promise case against John Jackett may be found in the *Falmouth Packet* newspaper, 3 Feb 1900, 9 Feb 1901 and 9 Mar 1901. Also see Henry Scott Tuke Diary, 8 Feb 1901 and 8 Mar 1901

76 Timothy d'Arch Smith, *Love in Earnest, op. cit.*, pp.109-110

77 Henry Scott Tuke Diary

78 G. Zilboorg, *A History of Medical Psychology*, Morton, 1941, p.425

79 Maria Tuke Sainsbury, p.174, and Henry Scott Tuke Diary, 16 Feb 1924

80 Hester Sainsbury (b.1890), Willy (b.1891), Geoffrey (b.1893) and Philip (b.1899)

81 Charles Kains Jackson, *Magazine of Art, op. cit.*, p.342

82 Maria Tuke Sainsbury, pp.118-19

83 *Cornish Echo* newspaper, 24 Mar 1899

84 *Chronicle of Art*, 31 Jan 1900

85 Maria Tuke Sainsbury, p.128

86 Henry Scott Tuke Diary , 6 and 7 Feb 1900

87 Maria Tuke Sainsbury, pp.129-30

88 Maria Tuke Sainsbury, p.131, has provided explanations for some of the delicacies offered: 'Pate d'Euchre' is game pie, and 'Plante Marine' is sea-pinks. 'Firefly' and 'Coeur Rouge' (*Red Heart*) refer to two of Tuke's own vessels; 'Menemopote' to that of his friend John Downing.

89 Wilson Lloyd Fox, *Historical Synopsis of the Royal Cornwall Polytechnic Society for 81 years 1833-1913*, printed by J. H. Lake & Co, Falmouth, 1915, Part 2, p.3

90 *ibid*, p.11

91 Maria Tuke Sainsbury, p.19

92 Henry Scott Tuke Registers (R257, R175 and R167)

93 Maria Tuke Sainsbury, p.71

94 Henry Scott Tuke Diary, 28 Nov 1924

95 Richard Ormond, *John Singer Sargent*, Phaidon, 1970, p.56

96 E. Bonning Steyne, *Studio, op. cit.*, p.95

97 Maria Tuke Sainsbury, p.106

98 *ibid*, p.113

99 Henry Scott Tuke Diary, 19 Oct 1899

50.   Berthe Tresidder, oil, 1918. R900. Berthe was the French wife of Sam Tresidder, brother of Hereward Tresidder, amateur artist and manager of Falmouth Trustee Savings Bank, and one of Tuke's cricketing friends. (Private Collection).

CHAPTER FOUR
Travelling On

In the summer of 1903 Tuke added to his collection of racing boats (the *Red Heart* and *Firefly*), a new yacht, *Flamingo*, again built at Jackett's boatyard. The *Flamingo* proved to be a great success, winning Tuke many prizes. One of her first voyages was a run to Fowey with Johnny Jackett and Alfred de Pass:

> a fair wind but rather rolly passage, carried the topsail for the first time. Strolled round Fowey and dined off cold chicken on board, with strawberries. All slept on hard planks.[1]

It is difficult to imagine the wealthy de Pass, who was accustomed to a life of considerable luxury, submitting without complaint to such an uncomfortable way of passing the night. One of Tuke's

51. Portrait of Alfred de Pass, oil, 1902. R363. (present whereabouts unknown).

closest friends and a constant patron, de Pass is now chiefly remembered, especially by many museums which benefited from his generosity, for being one of the most lavish art benefactors of the present century. He spent most of his adult life in England, visiting his native South Africa occasionally on business trips in connection with the family interests in sugar, shipping and the fertilizer trade, and only returning there for good when the Second World War broke out, to live out the remainder of his long life. He died at ninety-one, in 1952.

De Pass visited Falmouth with his family for the first time in the summer of 1895. He was sufficiently impressed with the town to decide almost straight away to build a holiday house there, and must also have made Tuke's acquaintance at the same time, as in the same year Tuke was commissioned to paint two family portraits. One was of de Pass's eldest son, *Daniel de Pass*, then aged four, which was begun in Falmouth and finished in London early in 1896, and the other—from a photograph—was of Daniel's great-grandfather, Aaron. De Pass's Falmouth home, Cliffe House, whose gardens then extended to the cliff's edge and could be seen from Tuke's own cottage, was completed in April 1897, and thereafter for many years the family spent part of each summer in Falmouth.

Tuke evidently taught de Pass to sail early on in their friendship. To begin with, he took to the sport with enthusiasm, buying first a Dartmouth steam launch and then commissioning from Jackett's yard an eighteen-foot racing yacht, named *Myrtle*, after his small daughter. Tuke was very impressed with *Myrtle*, racing her several times, and locally the vessel was regarded as the most serious rival to Jackett's own eighteen-footer *Marion*. After only eighteen months, however, by the end of the 1903 season, de Pass had become disillusioned:

> Won several races with the *Myrtle* this year but disgusted with racing as there was too much feeling, and people are always ready to suspect one of cheating, or do it themselves. Resolved not to race next year.[2]

He seems to have kept his word, as no further references to him racing or even sailing his own boat have been found.

De Pass's pique did not extend to Tuke, with

whom he remained on as close terms as before. Though de Pass could undoubtedly be difficult from time to time, Tuke possessed the rare gift of tolerance and seems often to have been able to maintain friendly relationships with people whom others found prickly or unpredictable. De Pass bought examples of Tuke's work over a period of more than thirty years, though many of his purchases were little more than sketches and the amounts of money involved were consequently small.[3] Tuke painted portraits of several other members of the de Pass family, including a small but delightful study of the youngest son John at the age of seven or eight; the portrait was to be especially treasured by de Pass as in 1923, when he was only sixteen, John was killed in a skiing accident on the Chamonoisaire mountain in Switzerland.[4] When Tuke's own health began to deteriorate seriously in the late 1920s, de Pass offered to take him to the Cape to live, in the hope that he might regain his strength in a kinder climate. Though Tuke declined the offer, saying that he did not wish to leave his other friends, it was not until after his death in 1929 that de Pass's regard for him was most touchingly in evidence. Determined that his friend should not be forgotten at a time when both the reputation and prices of his pre-war paintings had slumped, he bought many of the unsold works from Tuke's studio—and subsequently at auction the Academy picture *Genoa* for £16 15s which Tuke had sold for £128 in 1913—to present to public collections in his memory.

In Spring 1894, Tuke returned to London and immersed himself in the social life of the art world, going to the Artists' Benevolent Dinner where he met his old tutor from the Slade, E. J. Poynter, newly appointed Director of the National Gallery. At that dinner Tuke sat at Sargent's table between his friend Jacomb-Hood and the portrait painter Charles Furse.[5] Tuke embarked on a series of portrait commissions, using the Ennismore Gardens studio of the sculptor Gustav Natorp, a friend from their Paris student days. Natorp, twenty years older than Tuke, German-born and independently wealthy, was also a friend of Henry James and John Singer Sargent.[6] He introduced Tuke to London's fashionable society.

Thus in mid-May,

Frank Hird called, we went round to Kensington Studios and met Lord Ronald Gower.

And ten days later,

Dined at Lord Ronald Gower's and saw some of his many treasures.

Four days after that, Tuke having clearly been vetted and found to be socially acceptable,

To dine at Lord Ronald Gower's. George Wyndham and the Countess Grosvenor, Troubetzky, Lorne, Roussel and Hird there.[7]

Lord Ronald Gower was a popular figure in London society in the nineties. Fourth son of the second Duke of Sutherland, he had met Frank Hird, a young journalist and secretary to Lord Thring, a year earlier. Gower took him up and he was often to be found at Gower's London house in Trebovir Road. Evidently he was encouraged to find and introduce amusing and intelligent new friends. Subsequently Gower adopted Hird legally as his son; but Hird was more than just one of Gower's friendly young men. He wrote for the *Morning Post*, and was for a time its Rome correspondent; and in later life he published a competent biography of the explorer H. M. Stanley.

Gower was an amateur sculptor of some distinction, and had a few years earlier created the statues of William Shakespeare and four of his characters which are still in the Shakespeare Memorial Garden at Stratford-upon-Avon. Oscar Wilde spoke at the unveiling. Gower was a friend of Wilde, at this time a popular and fashionable playwright, though it was widely speculated that Wilde had used Gower as his model for the decadent aristocrat Sir Henry Wooton in *The Picture of Dorian Gray*, published three years earlier. Amusing, witty and well-connected, Gower was a 'man about town' who knew everyone, starting with Queen Victoria (who at his request wrote her favourite text into his pocket Bible: 'Love suffereth long, and is kind . . . Love faileth not'). His reminiscences[8] are peppered with the names of the leading figures in the London of the Nineties though he felt it discreet when he published them in 1902 not to mention his close friendship with Wilde, six years after the author's trial, and two years after his death in exile in Paris. The observant reader of his memoirs does, however, note how many good-looking guardsmen, subalterns and gondoliers attracted his attention on his travels; thus on meeting J. A. Symonds in Rome he records that

his faithful gondolier, 'Angelo' [sic], is always with him, a fine, rough, rather hulky-looking Venetian, who follows him like his shadow.[9]

52. Tuke and Johnny
Jackett sailing *Flamingo*,
c.1902.
(Private Collection).

On his side, Symonds felt an attraction for what has been called Gower's 'abandoned sensuality'.[10] It was on a visit to Venice to meet Symonds that Gower encountered Horatio Brown. Thereafter, Brown became a friend, and Casa Torresella Gower's Venetian base.

Of the other guests at that dinner party, George Wyndham was Member of Parliament for Dover, with a distinguished career ahead (in 1900 he became Chief Secretary to Ireland). Five years earlier he had married Sibell, Lady Grosvenor, the widow of Lord Grosvenor, and the youngest daughter of the Earl of Scarborough. Both were members of 'the Souls', that group of intellectual aristocrats who—as an antithesis to the dominant sporting and gambling ethos of the Marlborough House Set led by the Prince of Wales—shared interests in art and literature.[11] Another guest at the dinner was Prince Pierre Troubetskoy, the artist son of a Russian father and American mother, visiting London from his home in Switzerland. 'Lorne', another guest, was the Marquis of Lorne, Gower's nephew and protégé.

Though Gower remained an acquaintance, he did not buy any of Tuke's 'bathing boys' pictures. His first purchase, 1896, was a small picture of *Venus Rising from the Sea* (for which he paid £15); two years later he commissioned Tuke to paint his portrait (for £50) and also commissioned a sketch of Frank Hird (£5). Two years later he bought for £4 a sketch, *Playmates*, identified as 'with red shirt' (probably Johnny Jackett, since it is preceded in the Register by a picture of Johnny 'in blue shirt'), and a small marine picture, or possibly two, for £4.

A closer friend of Tuke's in London was Charles Kains Jackson. He led a respectable life as a London solicitor and in that capacity became one of the many sworn enemies of Frederick Rolfe, 'Baron Corvo', when Jackson advised his Christchurch client Gleeson White—later editor of *The Studio*—of Rolfe's financial instability. Tuke met them all on a visit to Christchurch in 1890, where Kains Jackson was then staying with his adored nephew Cecil Castle (who posed nude for Rolfe, and on one occasion, aged fourteen, had accompanied Tuke on a visit to Paris).

Tuke evidently liked Kains Jackson (they were almost precisely the same age), and in June 1890 completed a pastel portrait of him while he was staying at Pennance Cottage: Tuke gave it as a present to the sitter. He was to stay often over the years, with or without Cecil; and when in London, Tuke would often go over to Hammersmith to have dinner with Kains Jackson, usually on a Thursday evening, when they would be joined by other sympathetic and congenial bachelors.

Among the other guests was often the poet and dramatist Laurence Housman (though Tuke, not always very precise in spelling, used to call him 'Hausmann'). Kains Jackson had edited the *Artist and Journal of Home Culture*, a subtly homosexual journal in which he published in 1894 (under his pseudonym Philip Castle) an editorial on what he called 'The New Chivalry', contrasting

the Old Chivalry, or the exaltation of the youthful feminine ideal . . . [with] the New Chivalry or the exaltation of the youthful

53. Portrait of Gertrude Beldam, oil. (Collection a descendant of George Beldam).

masculine ideal . . . No animal consideration of mere sex will be allowed to intrude on the higher fact. A beautiful girl will be desired before a plain lad, but a plain girl will not be considered in the presence of a handsome boy . . . Of companionship also there is much to be said. Here it is enough to ask how much do ordinary engaged couples, how much even do husband and wife, see of each other? How much may not lovers see if man and youth, if youth and boy? The joys of palaestra, of the river, of the hunt and of the moor, the evening tent-pitching of campers-out, and the exhilaration of the early morning swim, for one pleasure of life and physical delight in each other's presence, touch and voice which man and woman ordinarily share, it is not too much to say that the new chivalry has, ten. Intimacy of constant companionship, of physical and personal knowledge is also a power of help and aid which cannot be put into words.[12]

The article caused outrage, and at least one sermon was preached against it. Two years later, after the Wilde scandal, it would have scarcely been possible to publish it. Indeed, it is ironic that one of Kains Jackson's friends and correspondents at this time was the Oxford undergraduate who became Wilde's fatal young friend, Lord Alfred Douglas.[13] There is no evidence that Tuke ever met him. And with the possible exception of Jackson's young cousin Cecil Castle (and he subsequently married), it is not evident that Kains Jackson had any sexual contact with boys and it has been averred that 'he disapproved of any physical extension beyond the aesthetic'.[14] The same may perhaps be said of Tuke, though his long-lasting friendships with Kains Jackson and Masson Fox (with the latter maintained even after his social disgrace, see page 84) must make his sexual orientation clear.

Tuke now had the entrée to London society at a number of levels; he could talk to many sorts of people, and although he was happiest at Swanpool living what he called 'the savage life', he also enjoyed good food and wines and the company of elegant women and entertaining men. Life in Falmouth was not always 'savage', and there he was prepared for any eventuality, as one anecdote demonstrates.

> He sometimes starts for a dinner, his immaculate evening-dress being covered by yellow oilskins. On one occasion, when he was living on his brig, he came ashore thus attired, bringing a suit of everyday clothes for the morrow's use tied up in a red handkerchief instead of the orthodox portmanteau. He had engaged to call for a lady to take her to an evening festivity of some sort. He therefore calmly deposited his bundle beneath a bush before presenting himself at her door. On their return later in the evening, he was indiscreet enough to reveal his hidden treasure. Next day an amusing story was freely circulating in Falmouth to the effect that he had used the garden as a dressing room, despite all his protests to the contrary.[15]

Though his life was now to some extent lived in compartments, in that he found himself at various times with widely different classes of people in a world where class distinctions mattered a great deal, it is clear that he treated everyone with similar courtesy, respect and interest. He would gladly listen to a Falmouth 'quay scamp' with as much care as one of his rich London sitters. He particularly welcomed as friends those who were similarly prepared to 'fit in'. One such friend was Lindsay Dening Symington. 'Symy', as Tuke called him, was at this time about twenty, and a frequent guest at Swanpool, with his friend the marine painter Frank Kelsey. Kelsey was a good

pianist and Tuke used to hire a piano for his visits.

Occasionally, Tuke used Kelsey's London studio in Roland Gardens, Kensington. But most of his London portraits that year were done in Natorp's studio in Ennismore Gardens, of sitters introduced by him. One was of *Mrs George Talbot*, Natorp's cousin. She had been a Miss Schlesinger, and the portrait (for which Tuke charged a hundred guineas) was a gift for her father. Her husband, George Talbot, was a regular soldier, from Co. Wexford; he would have appreciated Tuke since his sport, too, was sailing. Also at Natorp's Tuke painted twin portraits of Mr and Mrs Pidgeon: Winter Randall Pidgeon was a City stockbroker (Pidgeon & Stebbing). As a memento of the summer, Natorp produced a bronze plaque of Tuke's profile. Tuke responded by giving Natorp a sketch of Johnny Jackett.

Another lucrative portrait commission of this period was that for *Emily Kitson*, daughter of Sir James Kitson of Leeds. Tuke painted the portrait in Jacomb-Hood's Chelsea studio in Tite Street in the spring of 1896. He charged two hundred guineas. Tuke was subsequently commissioned to paint the younger daughter, *Hilda Kitson*, though Sir James's portrait, painted a few years later, was done by Sargent.[16]

[1] Henry Scott Tuke Diary, 30 June 1903

[2] Quoted by Brian D. Price, 'A Short Biography of Alfred Aaron de Pass (1861-1952): Art Benefactor Extraordinary', Royal Cornwall Polytechnic Society, 1981, p.9

[3] During Tuke's lifetime, the total sum expended by de Pass on the purchase of his paintings or drawings (most of which were family portraits) amounted to less than £300. Major posthumous purchases of Tuke's work made by members of the de Pass family included *The Message* (R152, 1890), which was presented by Mrs de Pass to the Falmouth Free Library (now in Falmouth Art Gallery), and *The Run Home* (R380, 1901-02), presented to the Royal Institution of Cornwall, Truro.

[4] Brian D. Price, *op. cit.*, p.12

[5] Maria Tuke Sainsbury, p.112

[6] Maria Tuke Sainsbury, p.111

[7] Maria Tuke Sainsbury, p.112

[8] Lord Ronald Sutherland Gower: *Old Diaries 1881-1901*, Murray 1902

[9] Lord Ronald Sutherland Gower, *op. cit.*, p.156

[10] Phyllis Grosskurth, *op. cit.*, p.311

[11] Jane Abdy and Charlotte Gere: *The Souls*, Sidgwick & Jackson, 1984

[12] Timothy d'Arch Smith: *Love in Earnest*, Routledge & Kegan Paul 1970, p.87, quoting the *Artist*, XV, 172 (April 1894)

[13] *ibid*, p.83

[14] Donald Weeks: *Corvo*, Michael Joseph 1971, p.317

[15] Flora Klickmann, *op. cit.*, pp.601-2

[16] *Dictionary of National Biography*: Sir James Kitson

CHAPTER FIVE

Edwardian Noon

The years between 1901 and 1914 saw the production of some of Tuke's finest work. It was also a period in which he was awarded some of the highest honours, culminating in his election to full membership of the Royal Academy three months before the outbreak of the First World War in August 1914. Though he had seemed to take the honour of election to Associate membership of the Royal Academy lightly, Tuke was well aware of its significance. He was now entitled to put work into the Summer Exhibition without going through the potentially embarrassing process of adjudication. From this point, annually until his death, there was at least one Tuke in the Royal Academy. Usually there were two or three, and usually a balance of portraits and 'bathing pictures'. He was pleased, also, when in 1904 he was elected an Associate of the Royal Society of Painters in Watercolour; it was a happy chance that he shared that election with John Singer Sargent. It was an acknowledgement of Tuke's eminence in that medium, and of the widespread admiration for his small watercolours of sailing ships. He was also highly regarded at the Pastel Society. In these first years of the new century, he showed regularly at the New Gallery, at Dowdeswell's (his first dealer-patron) in New Bond Street, and at the Ridley Art Society. Each year he provided at least a few sketches for the Falmouth Art Gallery, and his sense of filial duty ensured that he would also provide one or two watercolours for sale at charity bazaars supported by his mother at Hanwell.

For Tuke, it was a time of consolidation rather than experimentation; his style underwent no dramatic changes and he seems rather to have concentrated on perfecting the type of work in which he excelled and most enjoyed doing. Financial security undoubtedly contributed to a feeling of confidence. As one who could, had he chosen, have taken the opportunity to pursue a successful career in banking,[1] Tuke had always had a flair for making money, and entries in his diary during the first few years of the new century indicate that he was regularly investing in shares. Though his work was never to attract such high prices as that of some of his contemporaries,[2] his paintings were continuing to sell steadily to a public emboldened by official recognition of his art.

By now, in his forties, the pattern of his life was reasonably set. Early in January he would come up to London and—based at Hanwell—tour the galleries and take in a few theatres and concerts. He saw the greats of the day: Henry Irving, Ellen Terry, Beerbohm Tree, Forbes Robertson; and plays by the leading playwrights: Bernard Shaw, J. M. Barrie. His tastes in music were catholic but mainly classical: Beethoven, Chopin, Wagner. By mid-February he would be on his way down to Falmouth. In most years he would stay at Swanpool until early April, painting outdoors if the spring was kind. He would be in London for the first week of April, and then go down to Falmouth for Easter. He would take the train up to London, followed by his Academy paintings, in time to see them properly hung, and to attend Varnishing Day when positively the last touching-up could be done. On such days he would usually lunch with artist friends round the corner from Burlington House, at the Arts Club in Dover Street: it proved such a useful place that he joined the club in 1905, remaining a member for the rest of his life. 1904 was an unusual year in that he spent seven months away from Falmouth, abandoning his spring visit altogether, and instead touring in France and Italy. Generally in May and June he would be in London, staying with his mother in Hanwell, painting in the little studio he built there, or in studios—shared or rented—in Chelsea (a particular favourite was that of 'La Donald', Miss Helen Donald Smith), and then back to Falmouth throughout the summer, from July until late November or early December.

For his first year of Associate Membership, Tuke had been disappointed with his submissions to the Royal Academy, feeling that they did not represent him at anything like his best. Besides two portraits—of *Dr Henry Rayner* and his old friend *Horatio Brown*, painted in Venice the previous year (1899)—the main work was *Hermes at the Pool*, a painting with which Tuke had never been satisfied. He was not reassured when he saw the painting hung, remarking 'Hermes looks worse than in my studio',[3] and it was later said by Maria to have been destroyed. However, Tuke had not yet abandoned attempts to interpret allegorical themes, for in the following year he exhibited *The Coming of Day*, depicting a boy with outstretched arms standing in a wood at sunrise, the sun forming a halo behind his head, and at his feet a group of semi-draped figures emerging from sleep. In its lush sentimentality and the dream-like quality of the light, the

Facing page: 54. *The Coming of Day*, oil, 1901. R345. Georgie Fouracre was the main model, with Johnny Jackett and May Bull. (present whereabouts unknown).

55. Nude study of Charlie Mitchell, oil.
(Private Collection).

56. Portrait of Bert White, oil, 1902. R364. This painting
remained in Tuke's possession all his life.
(Private Collection).

57. *Ruby, Gold and Malachite*, oil, 1901. R374. (The Guildhall Art Gallery, Corporation of London).

painting (despite its rather absurd appearance to modern eyes) is closer in style than most of Tuke's other work to a type with which regular visitors to Academy exhibitions at the time would have been very familiar. In particular, a comparison may be drawn with an interpretation of *Diana and Endymion* by Tuke's former professor Sir Edward Poynter (by then President of the Royal Academy), which was commissioned in 1900 and exhibited the year after *The Coming of Day*.[4]

The theme of the sun as a life-giving force and an object of worship was one to which Tuke was to return several times (*To the Morning Sun*, RA 1904, is another example) and its importance to his philosophy was central. Tuke's Quaker upbringing had long since lost its hold over him and he had grown to detest organised religion, although he maintained the right of individuals to hold their own beliefs and while his parents were still living was careful not to express his opinions too forcefully in front of them. He defended Maria's later decision to convert to Roman Catholicism, but in his will he requested that no part of his legacy to his family should be used 'for any Roman Catholic or other specific religious or sectarian purpose'. Undoubtedly the slaughter on the battlefields between 1914 and 1918, which left few families completely untouched, strengthened his views, and it is no coincidence that it was during the War that he became a member of the Rationalist Press Association.

Maria wrote of her brother that 'he never made the slightest pretence of being anything but a pagan', adding—lest anyone should be given the wrong impression—'with all this he did not lack the divine spark of charity—no one was ever more tender-hearted'.[5] Paganism was fashionable in certain literary circles in Edwardian England, but Tuke does not seem to have had any direct contact with its leading protagonists, although they may well have admired his work. Despite Maria's assertion, two of those who knew him well during the first years of the century were convinced that Tuke held some form of religious belief; to Sallie Jackett he said of the area around his cliff-top home that

> when he watched the sun sink or rise [over Pennance] that meant more than all the churches and chapels in the world to him . . . 'that is better than all the sermons I've ever heard in my life'.[6]

If the repeated variations on the theme of nudes on beaches may be taken as accumulated evidence of his philosophy, it may be said that Tuke believed in a form of deism, a worship of the beauty and perfection of youthful nakedness drenched in sunlight in the glory of its natural setting. It is poignant that the golden invincible youth so idealised by Tuke, was to be so devastated by war.

The ugliness of war, if only at a distance, had already obtruded itself on Tuke's consciousness before the first year of the new century. Politically, as a committed Liberal, the controversial Boer War was repellent to him, and on meeting Horatio Brown in London soon after the conflict had begun he wrote: 'Glad to find he agrees with me in thinking the war unnecessary'.[7] In his diary, Tuke continued to record, with disapproval, the progress of the war: 'Flags, processions, and a most ridiculous fuss all day about Mafeking.' With his favourite model, Johnny Jackett, away at the war, some new names were introduced to the records Tuke kept in his Register of those who had appeared in each painting. Charlie Mitchell, who was soon put in charge of looking after Tuke's boats, and in later years became virtually his general factotum, made his first appearance in *Ruby, Gold and Malachite* in the summer of 1901—characteristically seen backview. His long back was a familiar feature of the many subsequent paintings over more than a quarter of a century, a much longer period than any of Tuke's other models.

Ruby, Gold and Malachite was well reviewed, and through the agency of Hugh Lane was bought by the City of London for the Guildhall Art Gallery. Hugh Lane had worked at Colnaghi's from the age of eighteen, and showing a flair for picking saleable pictures, had started in business on his own when twenty-three. Still only twenty-six, he was on his way to making a fortune as a picture dealer and expert. He was persuaded by his aunt, Lady Gregory, the founder of the Abbey Theatre in Dublin, to specialise in Irish art (he talked to Tuke about it). He became Director of the National Gallery of Ireland, but was drowned when the *Lusitania* was torpedoed in 1915. The City of London bought *Ruby, Gold and Malachite* for £350 through the great Alfred Temple, curator of the Guildhall Art Gallery, and the City's adviser on its picture purchases. The influence on the art world of such patronage was substantial, and could only heighten Tuke's reputation.

The other major Academy picture that year was *The Run Home*, a sailing picture on Tuke's rater, *Red Heart*, with Sam Hingston, Bert White and Harry Cleave. There were also portraits of *W. R. Paterson* and of *Alfred de Pass*. Paterson was an author who wrote under the pseudonym of 'Benjamin Swift': it is typical of Tuke's meticulous preparation that on the Sunday before starting that picture, he read one of Paterson's books.

Bert White was an accident-prone young man, whose frequent appearances in paintings between 1901 and 1904, often with his mischievous friend Harry Cleave, were due to a succession of minor injuries (some said to have been self-inflicted) sustained in the Docks Foundry where he was an apprentice fitter, causing him to be frequently laid off work. Among the pictures in which these two figures appeared was the 1903 Academy picture, *Noonday Heat*. Some years later, it is said at the urging of Leonard Duke, Tuke did a smaller watercolour of this picture in which the boy lying on his back on the sand is nude, and not, as in the Academy oil, wearing trousers. The watercolour is dated 1911.

Ruby, Gold and Malachite took part of its title from the marvellously clear green water which is the keynote of the painting. In this work, as in the incandescent *Noonday Heat*, no sky is visible. The shimmering effect of sunlight is created entirely with strokes of pure colour, tipped here and there with sparkling touches of white, using a palette from which all traces of black (*de rigeur* for all Victorian painters and their predecessors) have been excluded. Of the French Impressionists, Tuke admitted to admiring only Monet, but the influence of their theories on light and colour can be seen here to have pervaded his work, however indirectly or subconsciously. A painting in which the shadows on the sand, as in *Noonday Heat*, are composed solely of blue and mauve, and those on the flesh of orange and green, could hardly have been conceived in England even ten years earlier, and justifies Tuke's claim to be recognised amongst the front-runners of English Impressionism.

Charles Kains Jackson, in his 1902 *Magazine of Art* article, referred to Tuke as 'a born colourist, feeling the subjective mystery of colour almost as intensely as the objective reality of form'.[8] Writing from Venice nearly a decade later, the eccentric writer Frederick Rolfe (the self-styled 'Baron Corvo') bemoaned in words as evocative as Tuke's own paintings:

One thing which this world wants is some Tuke pictures of the Venetian Lagoon and . . . of mediaeval *gondoglieri* poised on *poppe* in Venetian canals . . . a painter like Tuke would have a free field here: for there is not a single painter of young Venetians . . . poised on lofty poops, out on the wide wide lagoon, at white dawn, when the whole world gleams with candid iridescence of mother of pearl, glowing white flesh with green-blue eyes and shining

hair poised in white air trembling like song in white light reflected in white smooth sea—of young Venetians poised on lofty poops out on the wide lagoon, at high noon, when all the world which is not brilliant is blue, glowing young litheness with its sumptuous breast poised in the air like showers of acquamarines on a sapphire sea with shadows of lapis-lazuli under a monstrous dome of turquoise—of young Venetians poised on lofty poops out on the wide lagoon, at sunset . . . glowing magnificent young strength dominantly illumined, poised in an atmosphere of lavender and heliotrope in tremendous stretches of sea and sky all cut out of jewels, limitless amethyst and far-reaching turquoise, or, all burnished copper splashed with emeralds and streaked with blue, the insistent blue of borage. No one does these things: no one sees them, but me. But Tuke is the only man alive who can do them; and he has not seen them.[9]

Tuke had met Rolfe several years earlier, at the Christchurch home of Gleeson White, an art critic who edited *The Studio* during the 1890s, at a time when Rolfe himself was struggling to become a painter. Tuke encouraged him to the extent of giving him a sheaf of drawings, perhaps to help him with the fresco he was then working on for the small Catholic church in Christchurch. However Tuke's acquaintance with Rolfe did not prosper—as Maria said, 'Rolfe was too fantastic a man to attract Harry much'[10]—or Rolfe would have been aware that Tuke had in fact visited Venice on three occasions (in 1892, 1896 and 1899), staying each time with Horatio Brown at his home Casa Torresella where Rolfe himself became an occasional visitor, attending some of Brown's regular Thursday evening soirées. It is strange that Venice failed to inspire Tuke—despite Rolfe's painterly description—to produce work of the quality of Sargent's sparkling Venetian watercolours or the moody nocturnes of Whistler, the two painters whom Tuke most admired and who both lived in Venice for a while.

This letter also links Tuke and Rolfe with Charles Masson Fox, to whom it was addressed. A member of Falmouth's leading Quaker family, Fox owned a timber business and also acted as the Russian and Swedish Vice-Consul for the port. This was not as much of a sinecure as it might appear, since in those days Falmouth was an important centre for visiting ships of many nationalities. Fox was one of Tuke's closest friends in Falmouth, the artist being a frequent guest at the home of Fox and his sister Ivy; and it was Fox who taught Tuke to play bridge which was to

58. The walls of Perugia, watercolour, 1912. (Collection a descendant of George Beldam).

Below: 59. Sketch of a Venetian gondola, watercolour, 1899. R315. (Private Collection).

Bottom: 60. Genoa, watercolour, 1912. (Falmouth Art Gallery/Falmouth Town Council).

61. Bathing group, watercolour, 1921. R982. (Private Collection).

62. *Noonday Heat*, oil, 1902. R382. (Tuke Collection, RCPS).

consuming passion in his later years. Tuke must have been aware of Rolfe's opinion of his work, so eloquently expressed in his letters to Fox, and it must therefore be assumed that he had no wish to resume their acquaintance. Masson Fox was one of the few people who tried, from a distance and ultimately unsuccessfully, to prevent Rolfe from descending into poverty and despair as he gradually alienated all his former friends in Venice; when, a few years later, Fox was himself involved in a scandal, having bravely decided to risk his reputation by appearing in court in order to prevent a blackmailing woman and her son from claiming further victims, Tuke refused to join in the general outcry of condemnation and loyally maintained their friendship until his death.[11]

On arriving back at Falmouth in the spring, not having had time to organise his social life, he would occasionally look in at the Boys' Club, and find out whether Masson Fox would be free to share supper. Tuke liked a busy social life, and it encompassed both sexes: he was equally popular with men and women, and his good-nature made him welcome everywhere.

A bridge-playing friend in Falmouth was May Bull—a descendant of the famous Packet ship captain John Bull, who had built the beautiful Marlborough House a fine Regency building on the outskirts of the town (he named after HMS Marlborough, which he captained during the Napoleonic Wars). With Mrs Manning, a London friend whose portraits by Tuke were shown at the Academy in 1901 and 1903, Miss Bull was one of a small number of mature women with whom Tuke seems to have been on intimate terms; May Bull even appeared, improbably, in the picture The Coming of Day. Tuke is rumoured to have considered marrying her, and was said to have been upset by her eventual engagement to Captain Robert Henderson, twenty-one years her junior, refusing to attend the wedding in 1911. After Mrs Henderson-Bull had performed the remarkable feat of producing a daughter, her only child, in her mid-forties, relations between herself and Tuke evidently thawed, for after his serious illness in 1915 it was to Marlborough House that he was invited to stay until he recovered his strength enough to be able to return home. Her daughter, Mary Seton Henderson-Bull, was the sole female beneficiary in Tuke's will, outside the family. May Bull was also a keen sailor, and was held in sufficiently high regard by Tuke to be one of the few people, apart from his recognised boatmen, to be allowed to sail his racing vessels. She had won the Ladies' Race in 1898 in the Red Heart, and she also sailed in the Flamingo and later, in the 1920s, in Tuke's Sunbeam Flame.

In 1901, the one-rater Red Heart was used in the foreground of The Run Home. The composition owed much to Tuke's fellow marine painter in Falmouth, Charles Napier Hemy—master of the depiction of moving waves as Tuke was of shallow water—who often used the same device of showing a vessel at an acute angle and masking off the top portion of the mast to convey the sense of rapid motion through the water. Unlike Hemy's more elaborately-planned studio paintings, however, The Run Home was painted almost entirely on the water, from the vessel Tuke had bought in 1892 to replace the Julie as a floating studio, a converted yacht with a glass-roofed deck which was known colloquially to the men on the quayside as the Piebox. The painting is an illustration of some of the sights of the inner harbour with which Tuke would have been familiar as he returned from a day's sailing, to 'make for home, passing close under old carved sterns, just clearing sharp jib booms and smiling figure-heads, and fetch[ing] up to our moorings with an appetite, and ready for another trip tomorrow.'[12]

In the background of the painting may be seen the stern of a large sailing vessel, the Norwegian barque Patria. Evidently Tuke had difficulty in finding exactly what he wanted, for the vessel was painted into the picture only a fortnight before it was packed up and dispatched to London to the Academy in 1902.[13] (The traditional Varnishing Day at the Academy was never used by Tuke for its original purpose, as it was his habit to submit works so freshly painted that they were still wet when the exhibition opened, and would not be varnished until up to a year later.) Though contemporary photographs reveal that Falmouth's inner harbour at the turn of the century was still crowded with picturesque small sailing craft, the larger barques and fully-rigged ships were becoming a much rarer sight. An innovator in much of his subject matter and methods of painting, Tuke was nevertheless a traditionalist in the matter of ships. He regretted the destruction of 'the romance of travel' by steam and easier methods of communication, and revelled in Falmouth's unique position as the traditional port to which ocean-going vessels called in 'for orders', 'where yet may be found some glamour of the old days of sailing ships bringing rich cargoes from strange lands, and fresh from the doubtful usage of wind and wave'.[14]

Tuke's cliff-top cottage was the ideal place from which to watch the arrival and departure of sailing vessels, even those which did not actually enter the harbour but anchored in the bay for steamers or punts to approach with messages or

63.   Tuke sailing his yacht *Flamingo*, 1906. (Private Collection).

64.   Portrait of May Henderson-Bull, watercolour, 1912.
(Private Collection).

65.   Portrait of Mary Henderson-Bull, watercolour, 1914.
(Private Collection).

66.   Portrait of 'Captain' Robert Seton Hooke Henderson, husband of May Bull, oil, 1923. R829A. The portrait was painted for his widow after his death in 1922. (Collection Michael Holloway and David Falconer).

orders for the ports of discharge. One day in 1900, he recorded with evident excitement,

> the great visitation of ships—the most wonderful I have ever seen. About 9 [o'clock] there were six four-masters at one time in the bay & six or seven other large ones carrying a great press of canvas in a light west wind. It came in wet with a strong wind about midday but they kept coming until 5 o'clock, about five & twenty altogether.[15]

When in Falmouth, Tuke tried never to miss the sight of one of these slow-moving stately vessels, and when possible to capture it in a small oil sketch or watercolour. These studies were, in his own lifetime, and have continued to be since, amongst the most popular examples of his work. Ship 'portraits' and studies of other vessels in the harbour formed the greater number of his many submissions to the 'old-established and select' Royal Society of Painters in Watercolour (RWS), to which he was elected an Associate in 1904 and a full member in 1911. On a few occasions, he was even able to travel aboard a tall ship at sea, in all its fully-rigged splendour, and the resultant paintings have a vitality which is quite different from the nostalgic views of ships at anchor seen from a distance.

In June 1890, for example, the sailing ship *Roman Emperor* put into Falmouth after a long voyage, on its way to discharge its cargo in Liverpool. The Captain, Alston, was a relation by marriage of Ayerst Ingram, and he and his wife invited Tuke to sail with them to Liverpool. He could not resist the chance of a voyage on a square-rigged ship, and accepted, sketching on the way. When they docked in the Mersey, the Alstons—who had hoped this would be their last trip—were asked by the owners to do one more voyage. They agreed, set sail for South America, and were never seen again. The loss greatly distressed Tuke.[16] In August 1899, though, he enjoyed the experience of being invited to sail on the old black-and-white warship *HMS Ganges* as far as Plymouth, when it was moved from its anchorage in the Carrick Roads where it had been a training ship for many years.

> Towed right up the Hamoaze with band playing & all the other training boys looking on. Quite a grand sight, in one of the last cruises of an old line-of-battle ship that will ever be taken.[17]

He enjoyed his occasional visits to Italy in the first decade of the new century not least because of the sailing ships he could paint. In 1904 he visited Leghorn, not far from the coast where nearly twenty-five years earlier he had first painted those lithe Italian boys on the beach; and typically of Tuke, he found himself encountering on the train a man from Forte dei Marmi who

> was tremendously excited when I enquired about Carlo and Eugenia Tonnini, Aristide Alboni, and Egidio Nardini, who were all his very dearest friends, and still living there. It was hard not to get out and go there, but it would only have been a disillusion, and I am glad I came on here.[18]

Leghorn provided him with marvellous subjects for watercolour sketches, 'quite the best for old shipping, and wonderfully coloured boats'. Then he moved to Genoa, where he found another old friend; a large British sailing ship, the *Lynton*, and its master Captain James, whom Tuke had met when he put into Falmouth a year or two earlier. In no time, Tuke was living on board while the ship loaded its cargo of Carrara marble for San Francisco.

> I . . . got out in the boat and saw a lovely late afternoon sun on the ships and pink houses which I tried to bring away with me. On Saturday morning out betimes and did a good sketch, which so impressed the 2nd mate that he sat gazing at it till his dinner went cold. We have a collie dog, two marmalade cats, a goat and a pig for company, with sundry birds, a German cook, and a new steward from Wakefield.[19]

Tuke returned to London in mid-May, 1904. His first duty was to visit the City office of the owners of the *Lynton* (no doubt with despatches from Captain James). There he met Archie Montgomery, son of the owner. Dowdeswell had arranged a show of Tuke's Mediterranean watercolours in his Bond Street gallery during June and July; there were fifty-five of them, and the show was a great success, with twenty-three being sold (which after the gallery's commission produced £203 for the artist). Tuke's other duty was to judge the drawings at the Royal Academy schools; there were 1300 of them, and he thought them 'a bad lot, this time'.

A few years later, in 1908, he had another chance to paint on a sailing ship at sea when he accompanied Captain James on another ship, the *Grace Harwar*, up the Channel, past the South Foreland lighthouse, and the Terschelling and Borkum lightships, as far as Bremerhaven.

67. *HMS Ganges*, watercolour, *c.*1899. (Tuke Collection, RCPS).

68.   *The White Ship*, watercolour, 1918. (Tuke Collection, RCPS).

69.   *The Run Home*, oil, 1901-2. R380. (Royal Institution of Cornwall, County Museum and Art Gallery, Truro).

Training ships had become quite a common sight in Falmouth over the years, providing both experience of seamanship and cheap accommodation for boys who were usually from poor backgrounds. With his keen interest in all aspects of life in the harbour, Tuke usually wasted little time in establishing contact with the commanders of vessels which spent any length of time in the port.

One of these arrived in Falmouth in 1905, six years after the departure of the *Ganges*, and remained a familiar feature in the harbour until after Tuke's death almost a quarter of a century later. The wooden man-of-war *Trincomalee*, a 5th-rater built at Bombay in 1817, was purchased by Geoffry Wheatly Cobb in 1898 to replace the *Foudroyant* which he was running privately as a boys' training vessel when they were wrecked off Blackpool in 1897. He renamed her *Foudroyant* when at Falmouth in 1903 for repair, and she came to stay in 1905.[20] The *Foudroyant* herself was not equipped for sailing, the whole of her top-deck rigging being missing except for one dummy mast. For this reason Tuke did not regard the ship herself as a suitable subject, although he painted portraits for Cobb of several of the boys who were trained aboard her. Tuke was a close enough friend of Cobb to be invited to be his best man when he married Anna Beach at St James's, Piccadilly, in 1921.[21]

It was not until after the First World War that Falmouth's most famous nautical resident made her first appearance in the port. The *Cutty Sark*, last of the great tea clippers, had been launched at Dumbarton in 1869 to take part in the annual tea race from China. In 1922 she put into Falmouth in a Channel gale, on her way back to Lisbon.[22] She was seen by Captain Wilfred Dowman, a retired sea-captain, who bought her in Lisbon, had her towed back to Falmouth, supervising her restoration by trained craftsmen there from his home at Trevissome, Flushing. Both Dowman and his wife became close friends of Tuke, who visited them in two successive springs in the 1920s at their Mediterranean villa at Rapallo. Along with his existing brigantine, the *Lady of Avenal*, which had been built in the tidal Bar Pool alongside Falmouth Docks, Dowman operated holiday training courses on the *Cutty Sark* for cadets intending to enter the Merchant Service. Her graceful lines offered one of the most beautiful sights of the inner harbour in the inter-war years.[23]

In 1927 the Falmouth Harbour Board, requiring more berths, insisted that the *Foudroyant* should be anchored fore-and-aft, instead of being allowed to swing free. Wheatly Cobb argued that *Foudroyant* being a wooden hull, while *Cutty Sark* had an iron frame, she needed more flexible conditions. Wheatly Cobb threatened to take *Foudroyant* away from Falmouth. Tuke drafted a letter of support, obtained twenty-three signatures, and sent it to Cobb with the message that 'if time permitted I could get any number of signatures. Those who have signed have done so with enthusiasm, and are representatives of many families and interests in Falmouth'.[24] The signatures included those of the Mayor, the Rector, Judge (Sir Arthur) Channell and his wife, and several important local names including H. E.

Cutty Sark & Fordroyant, Falmouth.

70. *Foudroyant*, left, and *Cutty Sark*, centre, at Falmouth, postcard, *c*.1927. (Private Collection).

71. Portrait of Peggy Hatch, oil, 1904. R475. (Private Collection).

72.   *The White Ship*, oil, 1902. (Private Collection).

73.   *Group of vessels and a tug*, watercolour, 1907. R558. (Tuke Collection, RCPS).

74.   Portrait of Ivy Hayter, oil, 1908. R609. (present whereabouts unknown).

(also known as *Sailors Yarning*), an arrangement of five men in various poses of relaxation on the deck of the *Mazatlan*, is made distinctive by the quality of the limpid blue light dappling the scene and subordinating its subject to the atmosphere. Tom Tiddy, another dockyard apprentice and friend of Harry Cleave, who appeared with him in *The Midday Rest*, recalled that all the models wore their own working clothes, supplemented occasionally with the odd nautical 'prop' which Tuke kept lying about the studio. Tuke quickly sold most of the paintings produced on the *Mazatlan*, several of them to local purchasers. Tom Tiddy also modelled for the smaller anecdotal oil *Foc's'l Gossip* and remembered bumping into Tuke on the Moor in Falmouth, then the site of visiting fairs, just after he had sold the painting. In high good humour, Tuke tipped Tiddy and his friends a couple of shillings each, which they promptly spent on the helter-skelter, the first time it had ever come to Falmouth.[25]

Harry Cleave was the principal model for the *Mazatlan* series. He caused Tuke a very brief problem when he underwent a religious conversion. Returning to Falmouth after his annual visit in May to the 'Varnishing', Private View and annual dinner of the Royal Academy, Tuke found everyone talking about the great Methodist revival that had occurred in his absence.

> Harry Cleave and Berty White both 'converted', Harry came out with letters, would sit if I particularly wished it, but would prefer not. So went out and did some rock studies.[26]

Luckily for Tuke, Harry's conversion did not last long; the very next day he wrote

> Shipped Harry Cleave for the week. Out Newport[h] & did a study. [On the Tuesday:] A hot day. H[arry] & sea pinks. [And in the following week:] Another brilliant day. H[arry] on the mizzen boom [of the *Mazatlan*].

Tuke was a thorough sportsman. At Swanpool his first activity every morning unless the weather was too bad was to dive into the sea for his morning swim—with those of his house-guests who chose to accompany him (and he tended to prefer those who did). Sailing was, of course, his greatest passion. When he took up cycling in 1895 at the urging of Jacomb-Hood, it became something close to an addiction: he wrote to his sister:

> Bicycling is now the rage. I have been my first

75. *The Look-out Man*, watercolour, 1908. R604. This is a reminiscence of Tuke's voyage on the *Grace Harwar*, painted later on the *Braemar* laid up at St Just-in-Roseland. (Tuke Collection, RCPS).

Croker Fox, May Henderson-Bull, and of course Tuke himself.

Both the *Cutty Sark* and the *Foudroyant* moored astern were visible from the window of the small cabin on Customs House Quay that Tuke leased from October 1903 onwards, using the room to store his sailing and painting equipment, and as a convenient shelter from which to paint on wet days, or simply to watch the comings and goings of vessels in the harbour. In May 1905, the French barque *Mazatlan* was towed in, having been dismasted in a gale, and moored alongside the Eastern breakwater of the Docks. The delay while her future was being decided enabled Tuke to go on board several times over a period of more than two months, and to produce several small studies as well as one of his most luminous larger paintings. *The Midday Rest*

76.   *Sailor Boy*, oil, 1924. The model is Joseph Parker. (Private Collection).

77.   *The Midday Rest* (also known as *Sailors Yarning*), oil, 1905. R544. (Private Collection).

fairly long ride this morning before breakfast, only about 8 miles out in the Constantine direction. It is like discovering a new sense, and I only wonder I have not done it years ago. Hood and Jackett and I now scour the country in company.[27]

Unlike Johnny Jackett, he never entered competitive races, but he proudly set down in his diary the very considerable distances he rode—in one case, eighty miles in one day, through Oxfordshire, Buckinghamshire and Middlesex. His first experience of motoring (other than in the steam car he had ridden in Paris a few years earlier) was when the Pidgeons took him out for a tour of Cornwall in April 1901. It does not seem that he found it a particularly congenial experience, and he never learnt to drive or owned a car.

'Ping-pong' was introduced in Britain in 1900, and Tuke played it for the first time at the house of his Mennell cousins in Albany Street, Regents Park, in January 1901 (later, he bought a 'ping-pong' set at Gamages and it was added to Cornwall's sporting pleasures). Tuke also played chess (often going with Kains Jackson to the London Chess Club), and Tiddleywinks (an Edwardian enthusiasm); and he was a keen player first of whist and then its variant, bridge, which seems to have been introduced to Tuke's Falmouth circle by Masson Fox. Tuke was also a keen stamp-collector, and his collection was substantial.

At Hanwell, he was an enthusiastic bowls and croquet player. But one of his greatest enthusiasms, first as spectator and then (in middle age) as participant, was for cricket. As a boy, he had played the game with his Stickney cousins in Hull.[28] Now, it sometimes seemed that his main purpose in coming up to London each summer was to go to Lord's and the Oval for county and test matches, and only incidentally to touch up his paintings at the Royal Academy. And again, having in 1904 spent three months in France and Italy, one of Tuke's first moves in London was to go to Lord's for the Middlesex-Nottinghamshire match. On that occasion he thought George Beldam (an amateur playing for Middlesex) 'dreadfully slow'.[29]

That was a somewhat harsh criticism of a player who was fast becoming a good friend. Tuke had by now become a familiar figure at Lord's during Middlesex matches. After such a match in the previous summer, he had found himself going in the same direction as Beldam, and they rode together as far as Ealing. Tuke never found it difficult to make friends, and soon

he was invited round to Beldam's home, Boston Lodge in Boston Manor Road, Brentford. It was near the successful rubber factory established by Beldam's father: successful enough for the son, though he was a director, to spend his summers playing cricket. He and Tuke had a number of things in common, though Beldam was in his mid-thirties when they met. Beldam was a pioneer sports photographer, and Tuke admired the composition of his cricket and golf photographs; Beldam was also a better than average amateur artist, and Tuke thought his watercolour sketches 'very good'. A few days later, Tuke was dining at the Beldams', and admiring more cricketing photos. On the next day he took Beldam round the Royal Academy, and a day later Beldam visited Lyndon Lodge and played bowls. Tuke produced a photograph of *All Hands to the Pumps!* as a present. Then seventeen-year-old Henry Allen, the son of the local vicar, arrived and (to his youthful pleasure) found himself playing cricket with one of his heroes.

On the next day, the glory was redoubled when Tuke and young Henry cycled to Lord's to watch the Middlesex-Nottinghamshire match; rain stopped play shortly before lunch, they lunched with George Beldam and then all went to a show at the London Hippodrome. Henry Allen was an endearing youngster (Tuke painted a poignant sketch of him lying in cricket whites on the lawn at Hanwell), and he cycled with Tuke round the Home Counties, to Windsor and Hampton Court. It was his first summer after leaving school, and he spent six weeks at Swanpool, crewing in

78. Ranji batting. A photograph of Tuke's cricket 'tutor' by their mutual friend George Beldam. (The George Beldam Collection.)

79.   Portrait of Ranjitsinhji, oil, 1908. R610 (present whereabouts unknown).

Facing page: 80. Portrait of
Kathleen Beldam, oil, 1917.
R851. (Collection a
descendant of George
Beldam).

81. Portrait of W. G.
Grace, watercolour. R1260.
This picture was painted for
the frontispiece of the book
Great Batsmen by George
Beldam and C. B. Fry and
was bequeathed to the MCC
by Beldam. (Middlesex
County Cricket Club,
London).

82. Henry Allen in his
cricketing whites, oil, 1903.
R1261. (Private Collection).

regattas, night fishing for conger eel, occasionally stripping to pose for Tuke, and bathing below Swanpool. Once he nearly drowned in a rough sea, and his life was saved by Tuke and Arthur Tanner, both of whom dived in to haul him out. It was a memorable summer, before he joined the London County Council as a clerk at County Hall.

For Tuke it was a memorable summer too. His friendship with the Beldam family flourished, and over the years he painted two portraits of the daughter, Kathleen, once as a young girl and once as a charming young woman. It was through his association with George Beldam that he became friendly with the great figures of English cricket in its golden age before 1914: W. G. Grace, F. R. Spofforth, A. C. MacLaren and 'Ranji'—Ranjitsinhji, later the Jam Sahib of Nawanagar. By this time cricket was almost taking over from cycling as a principal enthusiasm. It was in 1906 that George Beldam, holidaying with his family at Swanpool as Tuke's guests, planned and created a netted cricket pitch beside the cottage. Two years later, Tuke spent some weeks of the summer staying at Shillinglee Park in Sussex which Ranji had rented for the cricket season.

There Tuke completed a large portrait of Ranji in his magnificent Indian dress, bejewelled and turbanned. Ranji wrote to Tuke's family in later years:

> Very soon we all called him Tuko, for he had a most delightful personality and was a man well beloved by all of us. I am afraid I gave him very little help for my portrait, for I fought shy of sitting, yet I knew he understood. He had a gentle and lovable nature, and though a true artist he always found time to enjoy and enter into the hobbies and amusements of others, such as Bridge, Cricket and other sports. He will always remain in my remembrance as one whom it was a privilege to have known.[30]

Not many artists have the opportunity of private coaching from a leading test batsman; but Ranji taught Tuke how to improve his batting. Later, W. G. Grace brought down a team and Tuke's skill was put to the test. In the first innings he was caught off the bowling of Grace, for a duck. In the second innings Tuke did rather better: he made four. At dinner in the evening, one of the Indians wound a princely turban of red and gold round W. G. Grace's head; and on the following day Tuke persuaded the great man to sit for a watercolour sketch wearing the headdress. Tuke also produced a more formal portrait of Grace, and another of the bowler Spofforth, for books written by Beldam—one on great batsmen, the other on great bowlers. Tuke gave the originals to Beldam, who eventually bequeathed them to the MCC so that they might find their ultimate home at Lord's.

In winter, there was soon another pleasure, when Johnny Jackett was picked to play fullback for the England rugby team. On 2 December 1905 Tuke took Beldam and some other friends to watch Johnny play for England against New Zealand at the Crystal Palace ground. The All Blacks won, but Johnny distinguished himself and they were able to congratulate him in the dressing room afterwards. On the following Monday, Tuke noted proudly that the papers were 'full of good notices of Johnny's play on Saty.'[31]

'Ranji' proved to be a generous patron. *The Midday Rest (Sailors Yarning)* was one of four paintings sold to the Prince for his palace at Jamnagar, netting Tuke a total of £1121 paid spasmodically over a period of seven years. One of the others was *Return from Fishing*, which was a reversion to the subject matter and muted colouring of Tuke's Newlyn phase and is chiefly notable for the appearance of perhaps his only really successful female model, Isa Watson. Tuke had cycled from Hanwell up to Shepherds Bush early in July 1905 to negotiate the fee and arrangements for Miss Watson, a professional model, to come down to Falmouth. She spent about two months in Cornwall that summer, sitting regularly for Tuke on Newporth Beach, usually in the early mornings when the weather was at its best in an otherwise predominantly damp and windy season, and they were least likely to encounter interruptions from curious locals. Isa was the model for both female nudes in *The Pearl*, the main work to result from her first visit, which was shown at the 1906 Academy. Tuke was disappointed to find the painting being hung next to a 'raw blue sky' which made its pale morning light look insignificant,[32] but Isa herself was judged to be a great success. Later in the summer of 1906 she was in Falmouth again to sit for *Return from Fishing* and a watercolour *Beach Gossip* with Harry Coward, and in 1909 she paid her third visit from which two more bathing pictures resulted. *The Shell* and *The Secret Cave* were shown respectively at the 1911 and 1912 Academies. Sallie Jackett, by then engaged to Johnny and a regular visitor each summer to Falmouth, remembered Isa as a charming woman, who at Tuke's insistence always stayed with the respectable and hospitable Jackett family.[33]

Tuke's other major bathing subjects produced in the high noon of the Edwardian era included *Midsummer Morning* (RA 1908), *Gleaming*

83.   *The Pearl*, oil, 1905. R525. (present whereabouts unknown).

85. *Return from Fishing*, oil, 1907. R566. (Private Collection).

Facing page: 84. *Midsummer Morning*, oil, 1907. R593. (Forbes Magazine Collection, New York).

86.   Boy in a boat, watercolour, 1911. (Private Collection).

87. Sketch for *Midsummer Morning*, oil, 1907. R593 (Tuke Collection, RCPS).

Waters (RA 1911), *The Embarcation* (RA 1914), and *Low Tide* (RA 1912). The first three sold for substantial sums;[34] the last was burnt in the Hibernian Academy in Dublin during the Easter Rising in 1916 and Tuke eventually recovered about £70 in compensation from the British Government. In retrospect, it seems fitting that it should have been at the last Academy before the war that Tuke was awarded the highest honour of his career with his election to full membership of the Royal Academy, for there can be few painters who conveyed so evocatively the sundrenched and carefree atmosphere of life in certain circles in pre-war England. Many of Tuke's contemporaries felt that the honour was long overdue; after all, Sargent—whose monumental portraits have more than anything else perpetuated the image of the supremely self-assured Edwardian aristocracy—had been an Academician since 1897.

Even in Cornwall, others had achieved the honour before him; Stanhope Forbes had been elected an Academician in 1910, with Charles Napier Hemy following him the next year. In Falmouth the news of Tuke's success was greeted almost casually by comparison with the reception which had been given to his election as an Associate Member, this time meriting only a brief mention in the local papers. Of his closest friends in the town, who might have been expected to organise a celebration for him, the energetic William Ayerst Ingram—to Tuke's great regret—had died in 1913; Alfred de Pass was abroad at the time of the announcement, and had chosen to spend that summer at Perranporth; Charles Masson Fox was keeping a discreetly low profile following his public disgrace a few months

earlier, and Mrs Henderson-Bull was preoccupied with the recent arrival of her daughter, Mary. Of all those who rejoiced with him, Tuke took most pleasure in his eighty-seven-year-old mother's pride at having lived to see the crowning of her son's career.

1   Reminiscences, interview with Jack Hone recorded by Brian D. Price on 27 Oct 1962, p.17. See also Maria Tuke Sainsbury, p.23

2   The most Tuke received from the sale of a painting during his lifetime was £630, for *Midsummer Morning*, in 1908. By comparison, his fellow Falmouth artist, Charles Napier Hemy, received £1,200 from the Chantrey Bequest for his painting *Pilchards*, purchased from the 1897 Royal Academy Exhibition

3   Henry Scott Tuke Diary, 26 Apr 1900

4   Manchester City Art Gallery owns two versions of this painting

5   Maria Tuke Sainsbury, p.158

6   Reminiscences, interview with Sallie Jackett recorded by Brian D. Price on 30 May 1965, p.31

7   Henry Scott Tuke Diary, 14 Dec 1899

8   Charles Kains Jackson, 'Henry Scott Tuke, ARA', *Magazine of Art*, 1903, p.343

9   Quoted by Timothy d'Arch Smith, *Love in Earnest*, *op. cit.*, pp.68-69

10   Maria Tuke Sainsbury, p.91

11   For details of the blackmailing case, see *Falmouth Packet* newspaper, 15 Aug and 5 Sep 1913. Also see Timothy d'Arch Smith, *op. cit.*, p.129

12   Henry Scott Tuke, 'A Day in Falmouth Harbour', *Studio* magazine, 1894, p.78

13   Henry Scott Tuke Diary, 15 and 19 Mar 1902

14   Henry Scott Tuke, *Studio*, *op. cit.*, p.76

15   Henry Scott Tuke Diary, 3 Apr 1900

16   Maria Tuke Sainsbury, p.92

17   Henry Scott Tuke Diary, 29 August 1899

18   Maria Tuke Sainsbury, p.137

19   Maria Tuke Sainsbury, p.139

20   Reminiscences, interview with Cobb family by Brian D. Price, 1 Nov 1964, pp.8-12

21   Henry Scott Tuke Registers, above R752

22   Peter Kemp, *Oxford Companion to Ships and the Sea*, Oxford University Press, 1976, entries on *Cutty Sark*, *Foudroyant* and *Implacable*.

23   The *Cutty Sark* left Falmouth in 1938. See Reminiscences, interview with Catherine Dowman recorded by Brian D. Price on 10 Mar 1963, pp.13-14

24   Artists' Letters: Henry Scott Tuke to G. W. Cobb, 17 Aug 1927, No.338

25   Reminiscences, interview with Tom Tiddy recorded by Brian D. Price in Sep 1964, p.65

26   Henry Scott Tuke Diary, 7 May 1905

27   Maria Tuke Sainsbury, p.117

28   Maria Tuke Sainsbury, p.26

29   Henry Scott Tuke Diary, 14 Jun 1904

30   Maria Tuke Sainsbury, p.143

31   Henry Scott Tuke Diary, 2 Dec 1905

32   Maria Tuke Sainsbury, p.145

33   Reminiscences: interview with Sallie Jackett recorded by Brian D. Price on 23 May 1965, p.24

34   The three paintings fetched £630, £400 and 'about £300' (Register)

Facing page: 88. Two boys
and a dog, watercolour,
c.1914. (Private Collection).

89. Nude boy on a beach, watercolour, *c*.1920.
(Collection Michael Holloway and David
Falconer).

90. Nude boy, oil on panel. The model is Tom White.
(Collection Michael Holloway and David Falconer).

91. Seated nude on a beach, watercolour, 1900. (Collection a descendant of George Beldam).

CHAPTER SIX

The Later Years

Tuke's choice of painting for the traditional presentation by the newly-elected member to the Royal Academy's Diploma Gallery was curiously out of character, since it featured the first male professional model he had employed since Walter Shilling twenty-five years earlier. An Italian whose exotic colouring and exaggerated pose strikes an unusual note against the familiar grey rocks of Newporth Beach, Nicola Lucciani spent part of the summer of 1913 in Falmouth, at a time when Tuke's regular models, for one reason or another, appear to have been unavailable. Within a few years Lucciani was dead, killed in battle in the Trentino.

Tuke's nephews Willy and Philip were staying with him at Pennance when the news was announced in August 1914 that war had been declared, and though staunchly opposed to violence, Tuke seems to have been infected by their youthful enthusiasm and the general atmosphere of expectation.

> It is wonderful [he wrote] to have lived to see what is probably the greatest upheaval and disturbance in poor old Europe that the world has ever seen, and, whatever happens, the lives of everybody now living will be directly affected.[1]

As the first port at the entrance to the Channel, Falmouth soon became a focus of naval activity, with foreign ships thronging into the harbour for temporary safety, though to start with few people locally seem to have realised the gravity of the situation. The casual management of the war in its early stages is illustrated by the story that sailors from a German submarine were able to bring their vessel close in to shore, landing near Pendennis and visiting the cinema in the centre of Falmouth, before re-embarking and quietly slipping away, apparently unremarked by anyone.[2]

Despite Tuke's prediction of the repercussions of the war on everyday lives, his own way of life was on the whole affected less than that of most of his peers, and his paintings reflect almost nothing of the universal turmoil. One incident early in the war was typically turned to his advantage, when in September 1914 three large German sailing ships, followed a few days later by another, were seized off the Cornish coast by British battleships and towed into Falmouth triumphantly as prizes.

It seems rather mean to capture them like that, none of them had heard of the war until they arrived off the Scilly Islands, but it is all part of the horrible business.[3]

The fourth vessel to be captured, the four-masted barque *Ponape*, was regarded as an especially valuable trophy, being almost new, and was removed to a safe anchorage up the River Fal towards Truro, near King Harry Ferry. Tuke immediately seized the opportunity to obtain permission to go on board, taking with him two of his regular models, Charlie Mitchell and Harry Giles (dressed as matelots with pom-pom berets). Together with the ship's recently appointed watchman, the three were portrayed in a variety of situations which convey the bustle and activity of a full crew, something it would hardly have been possible for Tuke to achieve without his intimate knowledge and understanding of the workings of a large sailing vessel. The series of watercolours he produced also demonstrate, if any further proof were needed, the extent of his proficiency in the medium, each brush stroke placed with economy and precision, and the whole bathed in cool mauve autumn light.

Pulley Hauley[4] from the *Ponape* series was, with his Diploma picture *A Bathing Group*, the sum total of his exhibits in the first wartime Academy, although as a full member he was now entitled to have a minimum of six works hung. Tuke himself was not at the opening or dinner, for while still at Hanwell in the early spring of 1915 he had fallen ill with a severe attack of erysipelas, a severe inflammation of the skin sometimes called St Anthony's Fire, from which he nearly died. Nursed devotedly by his sister, helped by her mother's housekeeper, their cousin Ethel Rheam, and by Charlie Mitchell who had been hastily summoned—with the gramophone—from Falmouth, Tuke made a full recovery, but his convalescence was slow. Among many letters of commiseration, one came to Maria soon after the Private View from his fellow Academician Henry Pegram, who had three years earlier cast in bronze a bust of Tuke bearing an uncanny resemblance to Kitchener:

> Harry's pictures look very well in the RA and he was much missed and enquired after by his brother members. The President [Sir Edward Poynter] spoke to me quite feelingly about him, said how much he liked him, and respected his judgment, and how much they missed

94.   *July Sun*, oil, 1913. R766. (Royal Academy of Art, London).

93.   Study for Tuke's Diploma work, *A Bathing Group*, oil, 1913. R790. The model is Nicola Lucciani. (Sarema Collection).

95.   The *Ponape* off King Harry Ferry, watercolour, 1916. (Private Collection).

him on Council. One of my girl friends who is a student at the R A Schools said they all *loved* him in the Schools! Now ought not *that* to cheer him up?[5]

In another letter to Gotch written at the end of May, Jacomb-Hood mentioned that he had cycled down to Hanwell to visit him:

he seemed very pleased to see an old friend and to hear all the artistic gossip. I was only allowed twenty minutes for my interview by his sister Mrs Sainsbury. He looks remarkably well—fat and jolly with a grey beard and shaved head which with the skull-cap he wears makes him think that he resembles the late lamented G. F. Watts, RA. He is still in bed, except for a couple of hours daily, but hopes to be allowed up and out in the garden this next week.[6]

By July he was at last able to return to Falmouth, where he stayed for a month as a welcome guest at Marlborough House, as his devoted housekeeper Mrs Fouracre was herself not well enough to care for him properly at Swanpool. For some time he felt disinclined for work, and was not helped by the recent imposition of wartime regulations which meant that movement round the district was now severely restricted. 'We are now not allowed to go farther than this side of the Helford River and have to be in at 8.45.'[7] In addition, a permit was now required for painting out-of-doors, which did not arrive until the following summer. Frustrated by these restrictions, Tuke occupied himself by working on his only known sculpture. *The Watcher* was modelled first in wax and then in clay, and was only fourteen inches high; Harry Giles who was the model mainly for the head, with Charlie Mitchell's body, recalled that Tuke nicknamed it 'The Little Man'. He remembered seeing it set full of needles, the hands taking about a day to get right in the studio. After the plaster cast had been exhibited at the Royal Academy in 1916, several replicas in bronze were ordered but only five were ever cast; the recipient of one was told that his would have to be the last, as Tuke was not allowed any more bronze by the government because of the shortage of metal for armaments.

By 1916 most of Tuke's regular models had been called up, leaving him deprived in more ways than one, as several of them had acted as part-time boatmen as well as sitting for him when required. Charlie Mitchell in particular had become indispensable to Tuke, who felt his absence keenly until he was invalided out of the

Navy in the last year of the war. These were lonely years for Tuke, personal tragedy entering his life with the loss of many he cared for. Some fell in active service, such as Nicola Lucciani in Italy and Maurice Clift, nephew of Emmeline, who had appeared when little more than a child laughing in the shallow water in Tuke's 1911 painting *Gleaming Waters*; two cousins, Donald and Andrew Cruickshank died, and Alfred de Pass's second son, Crispin, was killed in his tank at Cambrai in March 1918. Others were taken through age or illness, including his old school friend Arthur Tanner, the artists W. H. Humphris and Charles Napier Hemy, 'looking very fine in his Dominican robes',[8] and his housekeeper Mrs Fouracre. Early in 1917, his mother at the great age of ninety 'ended her long and contented life in Harry's arms'.[9] The family took her body to Saffron Walden to be buried on a day of gently falling snow beside her husband. At every turn death touched the life of the painter whose brush had celebrated youth and vigour; even some of his portrait commissions at this time were post-humous ones.

Through it all Tuke maintained his belief in the precepts to which he had adhered throughout his career. Few bathing pictures resulted from the war years but those which did mostly featured a youth named Tom White, who in interviews and correspondence with Brian Price[10] has provided one of the best accounts of Tuke's methods of working and his relationship with his models. Tom White

96. Tuke painting Tom White on Newporth beach, *c*.1917. (Private Collection).

97. Tom White on
Newporth beach, *c.*1917.
(Private Collection).

98. Tuke putting the
finishing touches to *Lovers
of the Sun* in his studio,
*c.*1922, with *The Run Home*
in the background.
(Private Collection).

99. *Pulley Hauley*, pastel, 1921. R787A. This was produced for Jack Hone. (Private Collection).

100. *Pulley Hauley*, watercolour, 1914. R787. (Colmore Galleries, Henley-in-Arden, Warwickshire).

101.   *Getting the Canvas on Her* (also known as *Windlass*), watercolour, 1914. R785. (Private Collection).

102.   *Stowing the Headsails*, watercolour, 1914. R786. (Tuke Collection, RCPS).

was a Falmouth boy who was first seen by Tuke swimming with his friends in Sunny Cove. He was a lithe, slim boy and Tuke saw him as a potential model. The introduction was managed formally by another of the swimmers, Webber, a shop assistant already known to Tuke. Webber took Tom out to Swanpool, and once he had left school (at the age of fourteen) and become a Post Office messenger boy, he posed for Tuke over four summers, 1915-1918, and was his principal model while Charlie Mitchell was on active service. He appears in three of the Academy pictures of 1918: *Under the Western Sun, Morning Bright* and *Blue Jacket* and one of Tuke's most famous pictures, shown in 1919: *Summer Dreams*. He was paid 2s 6d per session, but sometimes as much as £1 for four sessions. Being a sensible lad, he banked it all and saved up about £80 with which he bought furniture when he married.

His account of being one of Tuke's models is disarmingly truthful.

Tuke never painted me in the studio, but always out of doors, usually on the beach, and always nude. My attitude to the whole thing was rather naive; I took it very light-heartedly. We were more like friends than master and man. I went or didn't as the whim took me. He would say sometimes 'the tide is wrong' or 'the light isn't right' in a cross way, then we would natter in the studio and he might put on a Caruso or Tetrazzini record. He was nuts on her — *Le Echo* I think was his favourite record. He might be touching up paintings and discussing techniques: the importance of clouds, sky, light being correct. My skin colour was important as Tuke did not want sunburn, and I could not sunbathe in off times.

I don't remember Tuke painting from photographs. I thought that being a model was not quite the thing, and asked Tuke not to paint the likeness of my face in a painting. Tuke accepted my wishes, and was a perfect gentleman. Often ideas for pictures came by chance. *Summer Dreams* happened one day when I was resting from posing on Newporth beach. I had probably been on night duty and was tired. Tuke said to me 'Do you think you could get in that position again? You were sound asleep!' and *Summer Dreams* was born. The picture was in his studio between exhibitions, and travelled all over the world. He was loath to part with it, and never did.

Usually we walked to Newporth beach for posing, but sometimes we went in the praam dinghy. HST himself would attend to the boat, which was pulled up just above high tide mark,

below the house, and do all the rowing and carrying if we went by boat, whereas I used to go along more or less as a guest . . . Tuke used to carry the easel and canvas, being afraid of me mishandling them. Usually we went about 10 am, and for a long time I walked both ways from home and back, but later Tuke gave me an old bicycle to use, which enabled me to get quickly to and from home (he himself always cycled in and out of Falmouth town). He would take an easel, oil paints in a box and canvas on a stretcher, involving some difficulty on the steep grass slope near the beach. I never saw anyone else modelling, I was always solo. Often when we had got to Newporth the sun or the tide was wrong, and we used to laze around, or bathe. Tuke got ideas for poses from those times. We were fond of diving in the deep gully at the southern end of the beach . . .

Tuke's studio was built of wood boards, with a big light in the roof. It was not dusty, and was fairly dry. It was stacked with paintings in disarray against each other, and he would grumble if anyone tried to tidy up. The cricketing had finished before 1914, but a concrete batting pitch was still there behind the studio, and he used to tell me of the famous cricketers who had been along there, 'W.G.' and Ranji. He had a bat autographed by them. He had a telescope for watching the shipping, and had a knowledge of the flags used for signalling . . . Once I had dinner by candlelight with him, just the two of us in the room of his cottage on the left of the front door.

He would often tell me where he would be going that evening to dine, to the Bulls or Foxes etc., and would ask me to go in with losses or gains when he played bridge. Of course I was not used to gambling and always refrained. Next day he would say 'Pity you weren't in, as I won so-and-so' but then he would give me 5s as he had a good night! Sometimes in the evenings he would go to one of the clubs, Athenaeum or Falmouth Gentlemen's Club, and play poker. Mostly he would win. He would ask me beforehand, would I like to wager 1s if he lost against 1s for every £1 he won. I never did, but he would often hand over two or three bob [shillings] next time we met![11]

Tuke tried to persuade the boy to stay in Falmouth as his model, but Tom White left for London, where he had got a job with the Commercial Cable Company. Once when *Under the Western Sun* was at the Royal Academy Tuke invited Tom White to Burlington House to see it and listen to the comments of the viewers. Of all the paintings

103.   Youth with oar, oil, 1918. (Private Collection).

104.   Sketch for *Summer Dreams*, oil, 1918. R898 (Tuke Collection, RCPS).

105. Charlie's back, oil,
1913. R762.
(Private Collection).

in which he appeared, it is perhaps *Under the Western Sun* which is the most triumphant; it is a sparkling study, an affirmation of the artist's faith in the pre-eminence and resilience of youth.

In his Registers, Tuke notes *Summer Dreams* as 'one of my best'. It must be one of the most erotic of his nude paintings, and yet (perhaps because) it is sublimely innocent. The beautiful boy—entirely unknowing—lies on the beach asleep. In later years, it was bought by a somewhat exotic schoolmaster at Wellington College and displayed in his rooms.[12]

That Tuke worked on his large canvases on the beach is well documented, in reminiscences and photographs. Precisely how much he was able to paint in the limited time available for each session in those conditions must be uncertain. He worked very fast, and one friend believed that 'the best things he did were all done in ten minutes'.[13] Tuke felt that the nude pictures were only effective if painted almost life-size, and was only once persuaded to paint one on a smaller scale.[14] But large canvases cannot be completed quickly. There is a clue to Tuke's technique, at least in the later years, in a description attributed to Charlie Mitchell.

The large canvases were not painted strictly out of doors. He used to take the canvas out before breakfast, work on it 'with pure turps', then he'd bring it back to the studio, and drop newspaper all over it. After breakfast he'd take the newspaper off, after it had absorbed the turps, and then block in the colour. In this way he worked quickly, and filled in later in the studio.[15]

Art critics sometimes joked about Tuke's 'trademark' in colour, the juxtaposition of red and green. But this was very important to him. Once George Beldam, staying at Falmouth, made a sketch of the *Jacqueline*, a grain ship with a green hull, and showed it to Tuke.

Tuke said 'Where did you see that ship?'. [Beldam] said 'It's in Falmouth harbour now'. 'Well, I've been waiting for a ship that colour for years!' and he rushed down and did several [sketches] of it.[16]

George Beldam, relying on the presumptuousness permitted to close friends, told Tuke that he wished the artist would paint something different.

Tuke replied 'No, when people want to buy a Tuke they want a typical Tuke'. That's what he was noted for, painting sunlight on flesh.[17]

Now that both parents were dead, Tuke had to decide what to do with Lyndon Lodge, the substantial family home at Hanwell. He still had a studio there, but had never lived there for more than a few weeks a year. Tuke's sister, Maria, and her husband were now settled in Hampstead and did not wish to uproot their growing family and move to the western suburbs. For a short period a caretaker was employed. Then the decision was taken to let the place, with Tuke retaining the use of the studio and a bedroom. The war was ending, and returning servicemen were looking for lodgings as they returned to civilian life. Lyndon Lodge was therefore let to four ex-servicemen: Rowland Alston, Leonard Duke, Jack Hone and Bernard Milling.[18] Three of them (Alston, Duke and Milling) had met as prisoners of war. Each of them had some interest in art.

Rowland Alston, a talented watercolourist, became Curator of the Watts Gallery at Guildford. Duke, a civil servant, an Assistant Secretary in the Board of Education, invested his army gratuity in contemporary watercolours, later extending his collection to old English drawings. Milling founded the Squire Gallery in Baker Street, which became a leading saleroom for English watercolours. All of them bought Tukes. Jack Hone was at this time trying to pick up his pre-war studies and qualify as a surveyor; but he abandoned that to become a stockbroker (in which capacity he dealt for Tuke, also acting as his executor). Tuke painted a portrait of Hone in his Royal Flying Corps uniform. The bachelors (only Milling married) set up a ménage at Lyndon Lodge, appointing a servant, and dividing the bills by four. When Tuke was in residence, the bills were divided into five.

In the summer of 1920, Tuke asked them all down to Falmouth, but only Jack Hone was able to go. Thereafter he spent all his summer holidays at Swanpool, occasionally serving as a model.

Another ex-serviceman to join Tuke's circle at this time was Lt-Col Sydney Lomer, who had been a regular army officer before the war (in the Lancashire Fusiliers and then the King's Royal Rifle Corps).[19] After serving through the war, he left the service accompanied by his batman, an attractive boy, Leo Marshall (Tuke painted him nude). Independently wealthy, Lomer had (under a pseudonym) published translations from the Greek Anthology before the war.[20] Even then he had a taste for flashy cars: in the summer of 1914 a boy actor aged fifteen, Noël Coward, was most impressed to be driven down to the West Country with a friend on holiday in Sydney Lomer's 'fast car'.[21] After the war, Lomer bought a house on the Norfolk coast where he held house parties, at least

106.   Tuke painting in the garden with Leonard Duke at Lyndon Lodge, Hanwell, c.1921.
(Collection Donald Rolph).

Facing page: 107. *Under
the Western Sun*, oil, 1917.
R876. (Private Collection).

Above: 108.   Ship with a
green hull, watercolour,
1907. (Collection a
descendant of George
Beldam).

109.   Sketch for *Under the
Western Sun*, oil, 1918.
R876 (Tuke Collection,
RCPS).

110. Group in the garden at Parkgate House, Petersham, Surrey (home of the Towseys), c.1921. Standing left to right: Donald Rolph, Stanley Towsey, Tuke, Colin Kennedy, Mrs Towsey. Seated: Jack Hone. (Collection Donald Rolph).

one of which Tuke attended. In the early Twenties he was a regular visitor to Swanpool, often accompanied by male friends. Occasionally the social traffic became oppressive in those years: large bands of friends would descend upon Newporth Beach to picnic, and occasionally photograph Tuke's models. One Falmouth boy recalls that Tuke

> used to curse them because they took up his painting time and brought huge hampers of grub. It didn't please HST at all.[22]

But Tuke was pleased with one introduction by Lomer. This was to Colin Kennedy, who had been a junior officer in Lomer's regiment. Kennedy, like so many young men emerging from that war, had no clear idea of what he wanted to do; and the England of 1919-20 was proving not very satisfactory as a 'land fit for heroes'. Lomer seems to have suggested that Tuke would find Kennedy useful as a paid secretary. Tuke liked Colin Kennedy, but was wary in money matters and was not willing to take on such an employee. It was eventually worked out that Kennedy would complete his studies at the Architectural Association school, and then became employed (by Tuke's negotiation) with the leading Falmouth architect, Corfield. He is remembered as a 'good draughtsman, but very untidy'.[23]

Another introduction in those immediate post-war years was Stanley Towsey, the quiet and philosophical English master at St Paul's School. Towsey, another bachelor, lived with his mother at Petersham near Richmond. At this time he was acting *in loco parentis* for a boy at St Paul's, Donald Rolph, both of whose parents had died. Donald Rolph, aged fifteen, was taken down to Swanpool, and became an occasional model: his head appears on the left figure in Tuke's Academy picture of 1924, *Lovers of the Sun*. In 1987 Lt.-Col. Donald Rolph MBE, still sprightly and swimming, cheerfully reminisced for one of the authors about those 'many happy days' seventy years ago: by the time *Lovers of the Sun* was shown at the Wembley Exhibition of 1924, Rolph was a Cambridge undergraduate and had to face some good-humoured teasing about being painted nude. Tuke, with Stanley Towsey, visited Rolph at Cambridge, going to see the Fitzwilliam Museum (whose curator, Sydney Cockerell, was a friend through his Meynell cousins) and sold a picture to the Chaplain of Trinity (Wilfred Ellis).

It was not always possible for Tuke's models to identify themselves in his pictures, because heads and bodies were used interchangeably and a figure might be made up from various constituent parts.

There is one curious instance in which a famous head has been included in a picture. Over the fireplace in the music room at Clouds Hill, the small Dorset cottage used as a base by T. E. Lawrence

Facing page: 111. *Facing South*, oil, 1920. R950. (present whereabouts unknown).

113A.   Sailing ship at anchor, watercolour, 1921. (Sarema Collection).

113.   Sketch for *Lovers of the Sun*, oil, 1922. R1023 The model is Donald Rolph. (Sarema Collection).

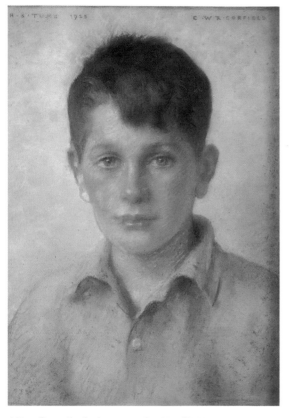

112.   Portrait of a boy, pastel, 1925. R1145. (Private Collection).

114. The *Margarete*, 1921,
watercolour.
(Sarema Collection).

115. Fishing boats,
watercolour, 1904.
(Sarema Collection).

('Lawrence of Arabia') when he was serving, under the alias 'Private Shaw', in the Royal Tank Corps at Bovington Camp, is a picture of a young army cadet sitting on a beach, with other boys bathing in the sea in the middle distance. The picture is described in the National Trust guide-book as 'an early painting by H Tuke of Lawrence as a cadet'. The one certain fact about the picture is that the head of the seated cadet is that of Lawrence as an adolescent.

One of Tuke's 1922 Royal Academy pictures was *Morning Splendour*, and his Registers describe it as 'painted at Newporth Beach in the great summer of 1921'. The next picture listed in the Registers is clearly an oil sketch for the big picture (17in by 21in, compared with 44in by 60in). It is titled *Picture of 'Gray'*, and Tuke describes it as 'An RGA [Royal Garrison Artillery] soldier seated on the beach'. (The Royal Garrison Artillery had been stationed at Pendennis Castle, Falmouth.)

There was a second sketch painted at this time, which Tuke called *Small Bathing Picture*. He noted that both pictures were sold to 'R.F.C. Scott' who has never been firmly identified. Tuke further noted that 'When R.F.C. Scott died "Gray" bought these two at the sale of his effects for a fiver!'. Brian Price suggests,[24] credibly, that 'R.F.C. Scott' could be Sydney Lomer — whose effects were sold after his death in 1926. 'Gray' may well be yet another pseudonym for T.E. Lawrence. Certainly the second picture was owned by Lawrence, for he gave it to Clare Sydney Smith. It follows from this that when Lawrence told one of his biographers, Basil Liddell Hart, that he ran away to Cornwall and joined the Royal Artillery aged seventeen at St Just in Roseland and that he served for six months before his father found him and bought him out, he may have been whimsically twisting Tuke's little joke — of putting the young Lawrence's head in a bathing picture — one turn further.[25]

Lawrence knew Tuke's work and admired it. Discussing art with a friendly Tank Corps corporal in 1923,

he was . . . most enthusiastic about the work of Augustus John, Henry Tuke and John Nash, but doubted whether painters like Orpen, Sargent and Lavery were more than able craftsmen.[26]

Lawrence's first encounter with Tuke's work was probably when in 1907, as a boy at Oxford High School, he was haunting the Ashmolean Museum. An Assistant Keeper at the time (he

became Keeper of Fine Art 1909-31) was Charles Francis Bell. At the Pastel Society in 1907 Bell bought a Tuke—*Bluebells*, a study of a nude eight-year-old (Georgy Williams) standing in a wood holding a bunch of flowers, and it was delivered to the Ashmolean. Through Bell's negotiation, Tuke was commissioned to paint a portrait of one of Bodley's Librarians, Dr Macray of Magdalen College. The portrait was painted at the Ashmolean. Another friend of the young Lawrence at that time was Leonard H. Green, an undergraduate at St John's College. Green and Lawrence planned to start a printing press together,[27] and Green hoped to print his stories about boys. In 1920 Green, with two acquaintances of Tuke's, John Gambril Nicholson and Laurence Housman, started a magazine, *The Quorum: a Magazine of Friendship*.[28] He was also executor to Kains Jackson.

116. Tuke in a dinghy holding a canvas, Charlie Mitchell on the right and Donald Rolph steadying the stern, c.1921. (Collection Donald Rolph).

The pattern of Tuke's year was now set. Colin Kennedy lived at Swanpool and acted as a general assistant (although going in to work at Corfield's office daily). Charlie Mitchell was Tuke's boat-keeper, crew and principal model (he married, lived in Falmouth, and cycled out to Swanpool every day). Charlie was very much Tuke's 'man-servant', although Tuke was obviously fond of him, and it has been said that Charlie had never been known to sit down for a meal with his employer.[29]

Housekeepers looked after the cottage. It was a solid and well-built Cornish house. To the left of the front door was a dining-room, its bookshelves holding the many silver cups won by Tuke in sailing regattas. To the right was a study, though Tuke was not tidy with papers and the drawers of the desk tended to be bursting with unsorted documents and letters. At the back of the house was the big kitchen in which Mrs Fouracre had ruled for so long, bringing up her large family (the room immortalised in *The Message* of 1890). Upstairs there was a large bedroom at the front, and a smaller bedroom for guests. The house-keeper and her family had other bedrooms at the back. It was only towards the end of Tuke's life that electricity was installed, and only for the last three years that he had a telephone. There was indoor sanitation, but it did not always work and guests had to disappear into the bushes. There was no bathroom; each morning, other than in very bad weather, Tuke went down to bathe in the sea.

In the evenings he would often go out to dine with Falmouth society, and play bridge or poker. Jack Hone recalled:

Tuke lived very simply—he was a most extra-ordinary contradiction. Down there he was prepared to live a completely simple life, but when he came to London there was nothing he enjoyed more than a really good first-class dinner.[30]

Lyndon Lodge, Hanwell was sold in 1921 and thereafter he made his base with his sister Maria and her family in Hampstead on his visits to London, frequenting the Royal Academy (where he showed at least one new picture each year) and the Arts Club.

1 From a letter dated 11 Aug 1914, quoted in Maria Tuke Sainsbury, p.153
2 Dr James Whetter, *The History of Falmouth*, Dyllansow Truran, 1981, p.70
3 From a letter dated 15 Sep 1914, quoted in Maria Tuke Sainsbury, p.153
4 The watercolour is in the possession of The Colmore Galleries, Henley-in-Arden, Warwickshire. A pastel version done for Jack Hone in 1921 is privately owned
5 From a letter from Henry Pegram to Maria Tuke Sainsbury dated 25 Apr 1915, quoted in Maria Tuke Sainsbury, p.155
6 Artists' Letters: G. P. Jacomb-Hood to T. C. Gotch, 29 May 1915, No.309, p.193
7 From a letter dated 19 July 1915, quoted in Maria Tuke Sainsbury, p.156
8 Maria Tuke Sainsbury, p.160
9 *ibid*, p.161
10 Reminiscences, interviews and correspondence with Tom White by Brian D. Price in 1971-83, pp.66-68
11 Reminiscences, interview with Tom White by Brian D. Price pp.66-67
12 T. C. Worsley, *Flannelled Fool*, Alan Ross 1967, p.135
13 Reminiscences, interview with Jack Hone recorded by Brian D. Price on 27 Oct 1962, p.18
14 Reminiscences, interview with R. P. Jones recorded by Brian D. Price c.1964, p.39
15 Reminiscences, interview with Neil Miners by Brian D. Price, 19 Apr 1963, p.43
16 Reminiscences, interview with Mrs Frank Connor (Kathleen Beldam) recorded by Brian D. Price, 1963, p.12
17 *ibid*
18 Reminiscences, Jack Hone interview, p.19
19 Army List, 1914
20 Timothy d'Arch Smith, *op. cit.*, p.248
21 Noel Coward, *Autobiography*, Methuen 1986, p.34
22 Reminiscences, interview with Tom White, p.67
23 R. Corfield, in discussion with the authors, September 1987
24 Henry Scott Tuke Registers, R986-8, note by Brian D. Price
25 For the convolutions of this story see Basil Liddell Hart, '*T. E. Lawrence*': *In Arabia and After*, Cape 1934; Phillip Knightley and Colin Simpson, *The Secret Lives of Lawrence of Arabia*, Nelson 1969; and John E. Mack, *A Prince of Our Disorder*, Weidenfeld & Nicolson 1976
26 A. W. Lawrence (Ed.), *T. E. Lawrence by his Friends*, Cape 1937, contribution by Alec L. Dixon, p.368
27 A. W. Lawrence, *op. cit.*, contribution by Leonard H. Green, p.68
28 Timothy d'Arch Smith, *op. cit.*, pp.138-141
29 Information from Ronald Smoldon, quoting Jack Hone
30 Reminiscences, Jack Hone interview, p.17

117.   *Picture of 'Gray'*, oil, 1922. R987. This picture, described by Tuke as of 'an RGA (Royal Garrison Artillery) soldier seated on the beach', is believed
to be a portrait of T. E. Lawrence, and hangs in the Music Room at Clouds Hill, Lawrence's cottage in Dorset. (National Trust Photographic Library).

118.   Ships at King Harry Ferry, watercolour, *c.*1920. (Sarema Collection).

119.   *In the Mangrove Swamp*, oil, 1924. R1104. 'Ralph and Manna in the boat'. (Private Collection).

CHAPTER SEVEN

The Run Home

Harry Tuke could never resist an adventure, or the prospect of a voyage. In the winter of 1923 he was invited to travel to the West Indies as a member of an expedition led by the explorer and author Frederick Arthur Mitchell-Hedges. He had lectured at the Polytechnic in Falmouth about his journey of the previous winter to the hinterland of Panama, where he had discovered traces of the ancient Maya civilisation. Tuke had met him, and found him good company. Mike Hedges, as he usually called himself, was at this time in his early forties, an adventurer in every sense. The son of a wealthy London stockbroker, he had determined to make his reputation by travel. In later years he claimed[1] to have made fortunes as a young man, first through poker games in New York saloons, then by speculation on Wall Street, and finally by friendship with the great financiers of the early years of the century—men such as Pierpont Morgan and Joe Duveen. As fast as he made these fortunes, he later said, he gave or gambled them away.

He spent some years travelling round Central America. In 1921 he returned to London to plan and fund another expedition. He found the authorities indifferent (not everyone believed his stories: later he was to be branded, in a vain libel action, a modern Baron Munchausen). Then—or so he told the story—he encountered an old friend on a platform at Waterloo Station, where they were waiting for the same train. She was Lady 'Mabs' Richmond Brown, a wealthy socialite, amateur artist and author. She was recovering from a serious operation, but agreed to finance his expedition, provided she could join it.

Hedges was an extrovert, claiming to hold 'numerous world records for the capture of giant fish'; his was the sort of temperament that Tuke often found attractive. Hedges was to return to Jamaica with Lady Richmond Brown, first to fish off the Black River in Jamaica, and then to continue his exploration of the Mayan sites. Tuke agreed to accompany them.

When he boarded the *SS Coronado* at Avonmouth in November 1923 Tuke looked forward to a pleasant excursion in the Caribbean sun, away from the damp of an English winter. Predictably Tuke got on well with the Captain and ship's officers and was allowed to sketch from the bridge. Anchoring off Port Royal in Jamaica, the party transferred to a hotel on shore, and after ordering summer clothing and being interviewed

by the local paper, Tuke found a bathing place outside the town and went swimming with a Marconi radio engineer and some apprentices. The temperature was in the high eighties and Tuke found the water 'too tepid for me'.[2] His watercolour box and cigarette case were stolen, and later in the journey he found that 100 dollars had been taken from a locked suitcase in his hotel. It was not a promising start.

With Lady Richmond Brown and her companion Tuke drove over the mountains to Black River on the west coast. He found it much more pleasant, and he was able to recruit models from the local Jamaican boys—Geoffry, Ralph and Arthur, and later 'Samwell', who 'looks like a fierce savage and is as gentle as a dove'.[3] The problem was that the heat was so intense that even these local boys could not bear to sit for long with their heads uncovered against the sun. However, at least two pictures were completed from these sittings, and shown in the Royal Academy in 1925; they were *In the Mangrove Swamp* (Ralph and Manna [Arthur]), and *Black River Boatmen, Jamaica* (Samuel and Ralph). From time to time Tuke accompanied Hedges deep-sea fishing, for sting-ray, spotted ray and conger eel. He spent Christmas Day sunbathing on the beach, an occasion spoiled by sand-flies. Later they moved to Montego Bay on the north coast.

In mid-February 1924, they sailed from Kingston to Belize, the capital of British Honduras. The plan was to explore the hinterland where Hedges had already discovered some ancient Mayan sites.

The author Aldous Huxley wrote an accurate description of this country.

If the world had any ends, British Honduras would certainly be one of them. It has no strategic value. It is all but uninhabited, and when Prohibition is abolished [the prohibition of alcohol in the United States was in force from 1920 to 1933] the last of its profitable enterprises—the re-export of alcohol by rum-runners, who use Belize as their base of operations, will have gone the way of its commerce in logwood, mahogany and chicle.[4]

The humidity of Belize is perpetually high, which means that everything becomes mildewed—including the official portraits of King George and Queen Mary in the Governor's House; Tuke was

120. *Sunny Hours in Jamaica*, watercolour, 1924. R1066. 'Ralph lying across the bow with the sloop *Energy* and the town beyond'. (Private Collection).

121.   *On the Fringe of the Caribbean*, watercolour, 1924. 'Samuel and Ralph on the beach under a tree near Black River'.
(Collection Michael Holloway and David Falconer).

asked to advise what should be done to them, and he made suggestions about varnishing.

Though he sketched incessantly, Tuke found the climate 'too hot and glaring' for paintings; subsequently he and his companions toured the Cays (offshore islands) in a chartered schooner. At Stann Creek it was blowing a gale, and Tuke was obliged to sleep on a camp bed in the schooner's hold, plagued with sandflies and malarial mosquitos. Accompanied now by another Mayan expert, Dr Thomas Gann, they sailed down to Punta Gorda, on the Guatemalan border, intending to travel up the small river known as the Rio Grande to discover a Mayan site that was rumoured to exist inland.

Tuke recorded his own laconic account of this awful journey.[5] Mitchell-Hedges later published a dramatic account which—allowing for Hedges' theatrical narrative—gives an even starker impression of its horrors, and a sense of the sheer idiocy of the enterprise. 'I stooped to folly . . . Of course we should have had more sense; except for Tuke we had all had experience of jungle life. Deep in our hearts we knew we were being fools', Hedges wrote with hindsight.[6]

They hired two dug-out canoes 'in advanced stages of decrepitude', crewed by three small Carib boys and two half-breeds. These were to be towed behind the expedition's motorboat, which would be taken as far up river as possible. At first they passed through mangrove swamps, then the going became harder and the obstructions more dangerous, until at one narrow point the second dug-out

> struck a log and rolled viciously, half filling with water. The tow rope gave a violent yank, shooting [Gann's] craft into the steep clay bank. As the bows struck, the boat rolled completely over, flinging Gann, Carib boys and all our stores into eighteen feet of turgid water.
>
> Gann scrambled up the bank, plastered from head to foot with thick yellow clay. Careering down the river went a heterogeneous collection of clothes, oranges, grapefruit, packing cases and grinning, woolly-headed Caribs . . . The vast majority of our baggage, including Gann's precious medicine chest and surgical instruments, was irretrievably lost.[7]

There was nowhere to land at that point, and they were obliged to sail on as best they could for a few more miles until they reached a clearing, with the remains of an Indian palm-leaf shelter. Gann and the two women took refuge in it, while Hedges and Tuke lay on camp beds beneath it. They had managed to start a fire but this provided little

protection against the hordes of mosquitos. Jaguars could be heard prowling around. 'Neither of us slept a wink', Tuke recorded.[8]

> The pitiless rain continued and towards morning the strain became almost unbearable. When dawn broke, grey and soaked, we looked a dreadful sight. We were bitten from head to foot, our faces so swollen that the flesh sagged beneath our eyes. To eat was impossible, but we found some tea and even without milk or sugar it proved a godsend. At daybreak we broke the miserable camp. Now it was light we discovered that . . . we were covered with thousands of ticks, each attached to a little mound of inflamed skin . . . So miserably we started up the motor boat and headed back the way we had come. Tuke's teeth were chattering and he looked very ill.[9]

Once back at Punta Gorda, they were able to take hot baths at the Commissioner's house, and rub themselves down with ammonia. To rid himself of the ticks Tuke had to wash himself with gasoline. He was at this time approaching his sixty-sixth birthday. It was obvious that he could not continue.

Hedges and Gann set off once again in search of Mayan remains, this time by land and on horseback. They did in fact discover the ancient site of

122. F. A. Mitchell Hedges (left), Lady Richmond Brown and Dr Thomas Gann at the Mayan ruins of Lubaatun, British Honduras (now Belize), of which they were concessionaires, 1924.

Lubaantun, and Gann wrote a scholarly book about it,[10] in which Tuke is not mentioned, though Mitchell-Hedges and Lady Richmond Brown are acknowledged as fellow-concessionaires of the Mayan ruins. When Hedges and Gann returned to Punta Gorda it was to discover that Tuke was seriously ill; the local doctor said that malaria had badly affected his heart. He sailed back to England on the *Coronado*, renewing his friendship with members of the crew, and doing portrait sketches of some of them. He also sold pictures to fellow

123. Detail from a cartoon 'Burlington House Burlesqued' from the Liverpool Daily Courier on the 1924 Royal Academy Exhibition showing Tuke's *Summer Sea*. (Private Collection).

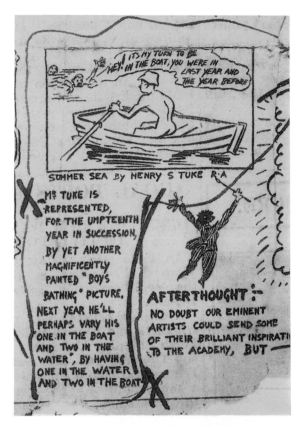

Below: 124. *Summer Sea*, oil, 1923. R1044. (present whereabouts unknown).

passengers, including Lord and Lady Lonsdale and Lord and Lady Mar and Kellie. Though he carried back with him a number of paintings, watercolours and sketches, the expedition could only be called a disaster, from which his health never fully recovered.

Landing at Avonmouth, he took the train up to London and was glad to be met at Paddington by his eldest nephew (and occasional model) Willy Sainsbury, who took him to the family home at 5 Provost Road, Hampstead. His family were distressed to see how ill he looked, but after a day's rest after the journey, he recovered enough to visit the Royal Watercolour Society and the National Gallery, call to see a new tea-shop opened in Regent Street by Willy, and have dinner with Jack Hone. On the Thursday, after breakfasting with Leonard Duke he went to the first Varnishing day at the Royal Academy, voted in the election (Russell Flint was among those successful) and satisfied himself that his own pictures were well placed. There were three oils, done at Newporth Beach the previous summer: *Comrades*, a study of two figures with a dog (Charlie Mitchell and Colin Kennedy and their dog Chippy); *Summer Sea* (Charlie Mitchell pulling in the praam); and *Beach Study* (Charlie again). Tuke's style was now so generally familiar that the *Liverpool Daily Courier* published a cartoon based on *Summer Sea*. There was also a watercolour of *Lady Richmond Brown* with a pistol in her belt, done at Black River during the expedition, and reproduced in her book *Unknown Tribes, Uncharted Seas* published later that year.

On the Friday Tuke packed and caught the midday train from Paddington. Colin Kennedy met him at Falmouth. There were those, among his family and friends, who thought that Colin exercised too much influence over Tuke in his late years. Before Tuke died, Kennedy moved out of the cottage and into the large and luxurious house of a wealthy Falmouth widow, who eventually left him substantial property. He drank heavily: he was certainly no sportsman, and never joined Tuke in his morning bathes, although he posed for him on many occasions. But his most important function, at least in the early twenties, is epitomised by the phrase repeated in Tuke's diary in those years: 'Colin met me at the station', was simply to be there, to be a companion. If many suspected him of battening on to Tuke and trading on his good nature, others recognised his genuine care and concern for the older man—Donald Rolph, for example, remembers him affectionately as 'a friendly, jolly character'.[11]

Tuke's activities during the six days after his return are typical of what he did when there was

125.   Youth in white trousers, oil. R998. (Private Collection).

126. *The White Ship*,
watercolour, 1928.
(Collection a descendant
of George Beldam).

127. Barque *Jorgen Bang*,
watercolour, 1899. R310.
(Tuke Collection, RCPS).

no sailing (the spring winds were blowing). On the Saturday, after watching a barque anchor in Falmouth Bay, he went to the bank, checked his account and collected the dividend vouchers that had accumulated from his stocks and shares during his absence. Jack Hone, his stockbroker, believed that he 'enjoyed far more making money on the Stock Exchange' than from his pictures. 'He used to get a terrific thrill if he made a profit on shares';[12] and indeed, Jack Hone was surprised to find, as Tuke's executor, that he owned a number of shares that he had never told Hone about.

While in the town he looked in at the new house built by John Downing, 'all beautifully arranged'. Back at Swanpool, Athelstan Johnson came to lunch: he lived at Tye Rock, Porthleven, and had bought one of the *Watcher* bronzes. In the afternoon Colin Kennedy's employer, the architect Claude Russell Corfield drove over with his son Roger, and took Tuke out for a run in their car. In the evening he went to the pictures, and saw the film heart-throb of the twenties, Rudolph Valentino, in his first great starring success, *Four Horsemen of the Apocalypse*, 'a splendid film', Tuke thought.

On the Sunday he had a lazy day, going to tea at Marlborough House with his old friend May Bull. Then he went over to Rosehill to talk to another old friend, Masson Fox, on his way to the Broad family for supper and bridge. The next day he was back to work, trying out different frames for various pictures. A group of visitors, including the Broads, came to look at his pictures. On the Tuesday he did some work on his Caribbean sketches; his heavy luggage (from the expedition) arrived from Bristol; then he went into Falmouth for tea and bridge with the Backhouses. On the Wednesday evening he was at a 'merry party' at Mrs Sharpe's.[13]

On the Thursday morning, with Colin and other friends, he left for London on the *Cornish Riviera* express, laden with gifts for his urban family: 'tulips, camellias, primroses &c' (they were from May Bull's garden), also 'eggs, butter and saffron buns'. On the Saturday he attended the Royal Academy Banquet, which was attended by the Prince of Wales. Tuke sat between Lord Rothschild and Lord Burnham. Later that week, he called in at Lord's to watch Hampshire batting, before lunching with the de Pass family who were on their way home from France. Later he took Charles Kains Jackson to the Academy, dined at the Arts Club and played bridge there. At the weekend he travelled down to Hampshire where a wealthy stockbroker, Gordon Anketell, was making a showpiece of Passfield Hall at Liphook. He held weekend house-parties where the guests were almost exclusively male, and Tuke attended several (he also 'weekended' at all-male parties with Sydney Lomer and his friends at Zetland House, Cley-next-the-Sea on the Norfolk coast).

So he filled May with visits to his friends, dinner-parties, bridge, shopping ('ordered boating and fishing gear and two new white sweaters'), cricket and the Wembley [Empire] Exhibition, where *Lovers of the Sun* was on show, and in the British Honduras pavilion, some of his Caribbean sketches. At one dinner-party he met Glyn Philpot and his friend and protégé, Vivien Forbes. It has been suggested that Tuke was out of sympathy with the modern artists of his day: Philpot was certainly controversial, but his *A Street Accident* and portrait of *Lady Carisbrooke*, shown in the Royal Academy of 1925, Tuke thought 'very strong'.[14]

By the end of May he was back in Falmouth, and on his first Sunday was able to bathe off Newporth Beach, his first sea-bathe for some six months. It signalled that he was feeling much better. He was soon out sketching ships in the bay from his boat *Nada*, whose engine, supplementing sail, gave him greater manoeuvrability but lacked charm. He was soon sailing in a new Solent Sunbeam boat, and was as successful as ever: that September, he won 'the big silver Challenge Cup given by Captain Dowman' at the Flushing Regatta. That was after he had done a good deal of work on the *Flame*, scraping and scrubbing her hull and revarnishing her. Tuke never shirked the rough work. There is a story that once when the Royal Yacht was in Falmouth, Queen Mary drove over to Swanpool and finding a man in rough jersey, old trousers and seaboots painting a boat on the beach, the Queen went up to him and said: 'Excuse me, my man, can you tell me where Mr Tuke lives?' He said: 'Oh yes, ma'am, go up the path, and the studio's at the top'. So she gave him half-a-crown, which he pocketed, and he ran round by a short cut and got ahead of her, tidied himself up, and received her. She is said not to have recognised him as the same person.[15]

Certainly Lady Mary Trefusis, one of the Queen's Ladies in Waiting, did visit the studio. She was there one day when Johnny Jackett's girl friend Sallie looked in. Seeing an elegant lady Sallie backed away; but Tuke, typically, called her and introduced her. 'Of course you must come down here,' she said, 'Johnny belongs to us all!' Sallie Jackett remembered that she was very young and embarrassed, but Lady Mary was 'a perfectly charming person'.[16]

By midsummer 1924 Tuke was once more painting Charlie at Newporth, and gladly recording 'a gorgeous morning . . . like old times'.[17] It was a good summer and autumn, and even at the beginning of November he was still bathing before breakfast. In December he dutifully went up to London to vote in the Academy elections, but the fogs depressed him and he returned to Cornwall for a further ten days (mainly of bridge-playing and going to the pictures with May Bull, to see Marion Davies and Norma Talmadge). Then to Saffron Walden for Christmas with his cousins, where he 'saw the new wireless installation . . . After dinner went up again and heard it in operation'.[18]

The London fogs convinced him that he must go to the sun. In January, after a few days meeting old artist friends in Paris, he was off to Italy, where the Dowmans had a villa at Rapallo. Tuke's room had a wonderful view of the bay; he got out his paints. He found time to visit a local resident whom he had not met for thirty years, the author and brilliant cartoonist Max Beerbohm. Then he embarked on a tour of North Africa, sailing from Genoa to Algiers. He found some good subjects for his sketches, and some interesting companions (including a French former rugby international who had played against Johnny Jackett). But then—whether from the food or heat—he fell ill. Back home in Falmouth, at the end of February, Colin met him at the station. He resumed work on

his portrait of the County Court judge *Sir Arthur Channell* which was to be one of his Academy pictures that year.

In 1925-26 Tuke painted a large 'bathing picture' at Newporth Beach, mainly from Charlie Mitchell, with one head contributed by a new model, Gordon Passell. It was 'like the old days'. *The Sun Bathers* was in the Royal Academy of 1927. There is one more 'bathing picture', *Aquamarine*, which shows two boys, probably on the beach in Sunny Cove, one bending down to pick up a blue shirt. It was shown in the Royal Academy of 1929 after Tuke's death. It is unsigned and undated, and probably the last picture he painted.

A major element in Tuke's work was his devotion to the sailing ship. There is a poignancy in the fact that the working ship in sail just survived the length of his life. He was fortunate that on his last visits to the Mediterranean in winter, he was able to capture some marvellous examples.

At the invitation of the Dowmans he went back to Rapallo in the spring of 1926. It happened that his good friend the St Paul's schoolmaster Stanley Towsey was also in Rapallo, but in the terminal stages of cancer; Harry Tuke loyally sat with him, inevitably finding the experience profoundly dis-

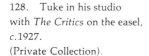

128. Tuke in his studio with *The Critics* on the easel, c.1927. (Private Collection).

129. The *Lady of Avenal*,
watercolour.
(Tuke Collection, RCPS).

130. *Just Arrived*, the
Bellas, watercolour, 1921.
R974.
(Tuke Collection, RCPS).

Facing page: 131. Portrait
of Sir Arthur Channell, oil,
1925. R1103.
(Private Collection).

tressing. He had been invited by an artist friend, Renny Stradling, to join him in the South of France; and after another visit to the incomparable Max he travelled north. He hoped to find some paintable ships in Toulon, but in Toulon it poured down with torrential rain throughout the day. They went on to St Tropez, then still a working port. 'Could see two nice Italian barquentines and numerous *tartanes*,' he wrote. 'This is the first place that has really excited me since leaving home.'[19]

In early 1927, having found a new housekeeper for Swanpool, Mrs Strout, he returned to the South of France, and to St Tropez. There, for the last time, he spent two weeks joyfully painting the ships.

> This place is just as paintable as I found it last year, only no sailing ships for the moment, but lots of the big sailing boats laden with barrels of wine. They are moored right in front of the hotel so I can sit on my balcony and paint all day long, but we go out as well on the Quays. The boats are all colours and are quite distractingly beautiful.[20]

The summer of 1927 was not very rewarding. The sailing was not good, and Tuke was only able to provide the Academy with one large painting, *The Sun Bathers*, and two watercolours done at St Tropez. He was now in his seventieth year, and was suffering chest trouble that sometimes made breathing difficult. He went to his cousins in Saffron Walden for Christmas but was not well enough to go abroad in the spring, after suffering a heart attack that February.

He went back to Swanpool at the end of March. Occasionally during 1928 he was well enough for Charlie Mitchell to take him out sailing and he did a small portrait of Colin Kennedy. By the autumn, after a summer in Falmouth, he was feeling better, though not well enough to travel up to London for Academy business. On fine days he would be taken out to sit in the garden, wrapped in blankets and rugs, so that he could look out across Falmouth Bay to the castle and the lighthouse. Sallie and Johnny Jackett visited him, and could see that he was seriously ill; they stayed with him until they saw he was becoming sleepy.[21] The winter turned bleak, wet and stormy. He lay in his bed in the Swanpool cottage, supported by his friends as best they could. They put his gramophone on the stairs and played a record that he especially loved: a chorister of the Temple Church, Ernest Lough, singing Mendelssohn's anthem 'Hear My Prayer' and 'O for the Wings of a Dove'.[22] In early February 1929 it was clear that

he would not live much longer. Colin Kennedy summoned Tuke's sister Maria Sainsbury and her husband, and Maria stayed with him until, early in the morning of 13 March 1929, with the last storms of winter lashing the windows of the cottage that had been his home for thirty years, he died.

He was buried in Falmouth cemetery, beneath pine trees on the hill overlooking Swanpool, and not far from Sunny Cove and Newporth Beach and Falmouth Bay, where he had found such joy, and enshrined so much sunshine happiness in his pictures for future generations. The headstone set above his grave was simply and elegantly lettered; a worthy tribute, as it remains.

Tuke's estate was proved at £35,840 2s 5d. By his will (made two years earlier) he left his household goods to his sister Maria, and his diaries to her son, his youngest nephew Philip Sainsbury. His intention was that Philip should turn them into a book, but he was not able to fulfil the challenge and a biography was eventually written and published four years later by Maria.[23] He bequeathed £3,000 to Colin Kennedy and £1,000 to Charlie Mitchell. To Lindsay Symington he left £300 and to Johnny Jackett £100; a similar sum went to Charles Kains Jackson. He left £50 to John Downing, Georgie and Richard Fouracre, the surviving sons of his longest-serving housekeeper, and to Mary Seton Henderson-Bull, the daughter of his close friend May Bull. He also left modest pecuniary legacies to the Artists' General Benevolent Institution, to the Benevolent Fund of the Royal Academy, to Falmouth Hospital, to the Falmouth Sailors Home and to the Rationalist Press Association.

He left his stamp collection (a favourite possession) and his pastel *Self-portrait* to Colin Kennedy, and a pastel of *Leander* to Charles Bell of the Ashmolean Museum. He gave his executors—his cousin Henry Samuel Tuke, Jack Hone, and his eldest nephew Willy Sainsbury—permission to give his friends any of his pictures or sketches they might think suitable, though he asked that his large pastel of *Leander*, which he long considered his best work, should be offered to the Tate Gallery. The remainder of his pictures were to be divided among Maria's children, though he suggested they should not immediately sell them, but wait for a better market opportunity. This was because six months before Tuke made his will, Sydney Lomer had died and the Tukes he owned, among them *Noonday Heat* and *Western Lad*, were to go on the market. It was during the 1926 coal strike and art prices were depressed: the Tukes would have been sold cheaply, which would have reduced the

132. Tuke's house at Pennance, *c.*1929-30. The main house is in the foreground, the billiard room (former studio) on the left and the later studio roof is visible to the left of the house.
(Osborne Studios, Falmouth).

price that could have been fetched. Tuke and Hone therefore bought them from Lomer's executors for £100. Hone kept *Noonday Heat*, and gave *Western Lad* to Charles Scott of Framlingham, senior partner in the stockbroking firm for which Hone worked. Tuke's advice to his beneficiaries was sound, particularly since he died at the peak of the 1929 world financial crash. The remainder of his estate was placed in trust for his niece and three nephews.

There were some fifty signed paintings and sketches in his Swanpool studio when he died, about twenty in the studio at Provost Road, Hampstead. Jack Hone thought that

he hated selling pictures, he hated even discussing selling them, even to his friends. All the time I knew him I don't think I ever had a cheap picture from him, I paid top price. He was very funny about selling. If anyone called

at the studio wanting to buy a picture he would dash out of the studio up to the cottage, and I would show the people round. They would say they liked this or that, and I'd say I'd ask Mr Tuke what he wanted for it, and I'd go up and show him the picture. He'd say 'Ask them 25 guineas' and after he would say 'I was very foolish, I should have asked 30 guineas'. He often thought he was giving things away.[24]

Most of the pictures remaining, including *The Diver*, *The Run Home*, *The Diving Place* and *Summer Dreams*, were put into a retrospective exhibition at the Cooling Galleries in New Bond Street in October-November 1929. They were reasonably but not too cheaply priced for the time (*Summer Dreams*, for example, was priced at two hundred guineas). In the following years, however, Tukes could be bought comparatively cheaply. He was out of fashion, and out of

133.   *Aquamarine*, oil, 1928. R1262. (Private Collection).

134. Two-masted white ship, watercolour, 1904. (Private Collection).

sympathy with the modern movement in art. His niece Hester once mentioned something to him about Augustus John, and he became angry, saying furiously that he 'wouldn't shake hands with that man if there was nobody else in the world'.[25] That sounds a momentary aberration, brought on by Augustus John's notoriously irresponsible behaviour to his wife and women friends; it is totally unlike Tuke to be discourteous even to those with whom he disagreed. Certainly he was disappointed, during the First World War, not to asked to be an official war artist (when Sargent *was*)—he was thought out-of-date in some official quarters. He was also disappointed when he offered his pastel self-portrait to the Uffizi Gallery in Florence for its collection of artists' self-portraits. He had the greatest respect for the Uffizi since he had painted there as a very young student. The Uffizi refused his self-portrait. The rejection was possibly even more hurtful because the gallery had invited a self-portrait from Tuke's near-contemporary from the Newlyn days, Walter Langley.[26]

Gradually over the years his artistic reputation has recovered, his rehabilitation helped by the Centenary Exhibition organised by Mrs Hilda Trench for the Royal Cornwall Polytechnic Society at Falmouth in 1957, and the exhibition 'Coming Home to Falmouth' organised by Catherine Dinn at Falmouth Art Gallery in 1985. The latter, opened by his cousin's grandson Sir Anthony Tuke (former Chairman of Barclays Bank), attracted national attention. At the same time, paintings of his were included in the exhibitions devised by Caroline Fox and Francis Greenacre that revived interest in the work of the Newlyn School, first in Newlyn and then in Plymouth, Bristol, and at the Barbican Art Gallery in the City of London in 1979 and 1985.

The cottage at Swanpool remained. Mrs Strout, Tuke's last housekeeper, stayed on as the Fox family's tenant for a further twenty years, bringing up her family there through the Second World War. The ground was honeycombed with tunnels from the old eighteenth century nitrite mines; and in the 1950s there was further tunnelling to provide an exit point through the cliffs for a sewer pipe. The explosives used in tunnelling rocked the cottage and caused a cliff fall in front of it, adding to the effects of the erosion by the sea. Mrs Strout was afraid to stay, and moved out. The cottage remained empty and derelict for a few years, and following a compulsory demolition order from the council it was pulled down.

Today the shape of the old cricket pitch where Tuke once batted to enthusiastic bowling may be roughly discerned among the wild flowers on the windswept cliff of Pennance. Not much else remains to mark the cottage, though the strip of shingle below it is still known to local people as 'Tuke's beach'. In the height of summer the roar of motorboats towing water-skiers breaks the calm of Falmouth Bay. But from time to time the billowing sails of racing yachts may still be seen tacking and cross-tacking beneath Pendennis Castle; and on summer mornings the boys of Falmouth, if unobserved, climb down the cliff path to Sunny Cove and Newporth Beach to dive into a sea that is as translucent, blue-green and timelessly beautiful as it was when captured in the paintings, watercolours and pastels of Henry Scott Tuke.

1 F. A. Mitchell-Hedges; *Danger My Ally*, Elek Books, 1954 (this book was written many years after the event, and contains many inaccuracies: Hedges evidently forgot, for example, that Tuke was fishing with them at the Black River)

2 Henry Scott Tuke Diary, 10 Dec 1923

3 Henry Scott Tuke Diary, 4 Jan 1924

4 Aldous Huxley, *Beyond the Mexique Bay*, Chatto & Windus, 1934, p.35

5 Henry Scott Tuke Diary: 10-11 Mar 1924

6 Mitchell-Hedges, *op. cit.*, p.165

7 Mitchell-Hedges, *op. cit.*, p.167

8 Henry Scott Tuke Diary, 11 Mar 1924

9 Mitchell-Hedges, *op. cit.*, p.168

10 Thomas Gann, *Mystery Cities, Exploration and Adventure in Lubaantun*, Duckworth, 1925

11 Reminiscences, *op. cit.*, p.52

12 Reminiscences, *op. cit.*, p.17

13 Henry Scott Tuke Diary: 24-31 April 1924

14 Henry Scott Tuke Diary: 24 April 1924

15 Reminiscences, *op. cit.*, p.40

16 Reminiscences, *op. cit.*, p.31

17 Henry Scott Tuke Diary: 15 July 1924

18 Henry Scott Tuke Diary: 25 Dec 1924

19 Maria Tuke Sainsbury, p.176

20 Maria Tuke Sainsbury, p.177

21 Reminiscences, interview with Sallie Jackett, p.28

22 Information from the daughter of Tuke's housekeeper to Brian Price

23 Maria Tuke Sainsbury

24 Reminiscences, interview with Jack Hone, p.18

25 Reminiscences, interview with Hester Sainsbury by Brian D. Price, *c*.1960s, p.57

26 C. Fox and F. Greenacre: *Painting in Newlyn*, Barbican Art Gallery, p.63

135. Henry Scott Tuke. Photograph. (Private Collection).

136. Gorse bushes,
Falmouth, watercolour,
1921.
(Collection a descendant of
George Beldam).

137. San Tropez,
watercolour.
(Private Collection).

A Day in Falmouth Harbour *by Henry Scott Tuke*

In these days, when almost every one who has crossed the Channel publishes his reminiscences, when steam and easy communication have done so much to destroy the romance of travel, it is something to be thankful for to know of a place in England where yet may be found some glamour of the old days of sailing ships bringing rich cargoes from strange lands, and fresh from the doubtful usage of wind and wave.

That such a place does exist will be readily admitted by any one who will undertake the troublesome journey (and troublesome it is) from London to the south-west corner of our island, and bring up at Falmouth. Though the number of vessels calling here is nothing to what it was twenty years ago, there are still plenty to be a continual source of interest and to give the town a curious cosmopolitan air, making the inhabitants, too, feel in close touch with foreign countries; although nothing will ever persuade a Cornishman to think highly of Italians—a nation who feed on its own despised salt pilchards.

Let us go down through the narrow street to take a boat at the quay, passing on our way numerous marine stores and inns kept by Germans, Swedes and Norwegians, and meeting knots of sauntering sailors, in many coloured coats, jabbering in every European tongue. The wind is light from the W.S.W. as we slip from the moorings and glide out from the inner harbour. This ought to be a good day to see the finest sight our port can offer—the arrival of a homeward-bounder, all travel-stained and weather-beaten, now first sighting land after a voyage of perhaps three or four months.

This seems to be the case, for a vessel has just brought up in the Roads, with a swarm of small steamers and boats buzzing round her; but we will leave the Custom House officer to examine her and make for the harbour mouth.

As we clear the Castle head and get out into the open, the wind freshens, and the Londoner recognises that this is no pleasure trip on the Welsh Harp or Serpentine, but real sea sailing. Our course is for the Manacles, the westerly boundary of the bay. This being about six miles distant we have leisure to take note of our boat, which is a good specimen of a class well known among boating men by the local name of 'quay punt'. She is 32 feet long, with a 10-inch [*sic*] beam and draws about 6 inches [*sic*].* She has a mainsail, foresail and mizzen, is easily handled,

safe, and a hard goer, and her equal is not to be found on the coast.

Arrived off the Manacle bell buoy, there seems at first nothing particular to see beyond a coaster or two running up and a large vessel, hull down, going up Channel. But presently sharp eyes discover a little vague blot, warmer in colour than the grey sky, and a square-rigged vessel is faintly but certainly made out. The tide and wind being favourable, she begins quickly to loom up bigger, a tug and quay punt being already in attendance.

We wait for another hour, and turn to run up with the new-comer. Now out with your note-books, you painters (and poets, if you happen to work from Nature), for you may go long before you have a finer theme than this—a white Italian ship in full sail; the old flag of red, white and green flutters from the mizzen, her misty sides and bellying canvas tower above you, and dark faces peer from behind rigging, ropes and chains. Glad are they to look on fresh fellow-men after the monotony of a long sojourn with the same people; but they have little time to be sentimental, for now they are ordered aloft, and, fortunately for us, the vessel quickly begins to take in sail, so that we can easily keep our distance ahead of her. As we near the harbour mouth a little vermilion steamer comes cutting her way through the grey-green water, and the boarding clerks nimbly jump on board with letters and papers. Sometimes they bring orders for the port of discharge, in which case the vessel will perhaps square away up Channel and never enter the harbour. But this time she comes right on, the pilot skilfully threading his way through the already crowded Roads till he finds a berth high up by the old training ship. With a roar that can be heard all over the harbour the anchor and chain run out, and as she swings to the wind we leave our ship and make for home, passing close under old carved sterns, just clearing sharp jib-booms and smiling figure-heads, and fetch up to our moorings with an appetite, and ready for another trip tomorrow.   H.S.T.

(From the *Studio*, Vol 3, 1894, pp. 76-78)

*Note: As printed in the *Studio*, the dimensions there given are '32 feet long, with a 10-inch beam, and draws about 6 inches'. The last two measurements must be wrong, since a '10-inch' beam would give a configuration like a racing eight, and Falmouth quay punts were ocean-going and so had a draught measured in feet, not inches.

Poems *by Horatio Brown*

Johnnie Jacket

Hie! Johnnie Jacket!
Ho! Johnnie Jacket!
Young Johnnie Jacket,
Come and sail wi' me;
For there she lies at anchor,
The 'Fire Queen', the spanker,
And the tide is like a millrace by Penmawr and out to sea.

Hie! Johnnie Jacket!
Ho! Johnnie Jacket!
Lad Johnnie Jacket,
Come and bathe wi' me;
For the water's all a-bubble,
A-churn, a-moil, a-trouble,
Where the breakers come a-rolling in the cove below Penlee.

Hie! Johnnie Jacket!
Ho! Johnnie Jacket!
Young Johnnie Jacket,
Come and live wi' me;
For life may be a folly,
But we two will make it jolly,
If we sail and swim together, and can live like you and me.

Pennance

So grey, so cold this broad expanse of sea!
So pallid green and brown the barren lea!
So sternly piled, so ominously black
These cliffs that beetle o'er the wind-strewn wrack!
Ah! who could guess that this indeed would prove
The radiant home of such thrice-lovely love?

Yet so it is. Come tempest, storm or rain!
Beat breakers, surging from a shoreless main!
Howl winds by night and fling the flying foam
Against the windows of that cliff-built home!
Triumphant as yon beacon fires that glow
Athwart the ceaseless turmoil, ebb and flow,
This love serene, erect, robust and grand,
Guides all true lovers to this true love's land.

(From *Drift*, Verses by Horatio F Brown, Grant Richards, 1900)

Sonnet *from* The Artist

No. 1076

Youth, beautiful and daring, and divine,
    Loved of the Gods, when yet the happy earth
    Was joyful in its mourning and new birth;
When yet the very odours of the brine
Love's cradle, filled with sweetness all the shrine
    Of Venus, ere these starveling times of dearth,
    Of priest-praised abstinence, made void of mirth,
Had given us water where we asked for wine.

Youth, standing sweet, triumphant by the sea
    All freshness of the day and all the light
    Of morn on thy white limbs, firm, bared and bright
For conflict, and assured of victory,
Youth, make one conquest more; and take again
    Thy rightful crown, in lovers' hearts to reign!

Pasted in Tuke's Registers on the page referring to *Perseus
and Andromeda* (R121). Charles Kains Jackson told the
anthologist S. E. Cottam that a sonnet in the *Artist* of 1889
was by Henry Scott Tuke. This seems to be the poem to
which he referred, though its authorship cannot be firmly
attributed.

Index of Names

The page numbers given in italics refer to those on which illustrations appear.

An asterisk denotes one of Tuke's models.